Best Careers
for Bilingual
Latinos

MAR 1999
Co

AGM 7957-1

Best Careers
for Bilingual
Latinos

Market Your Fluency
in Spanish
to Get Ahead on the Job

Graciela Kenig

VGM Career Horizons
NTC/Contemporary Publishing Group

Library of Congress Cataloging-in-Publication Data

Kenig, Graciela.
 Best careers for bilingual Latinos : market your fluency in Spanish
to get ahead on the job / Graciela Kenig.
  p.   cm.
 ISBN 0-8442-4541-0
  1. Vocational guidance—United States.   2. Hispanic Americans—
Employment—United States.   3. Bilingualism—United States.
4. Spanish-language—Vocational guidance—United States   I. Title.
HF5382.5.U5K455   1998
331.7′02′08968073—dc21   98-30744
                                                                                CIP

Published by VGM Career Books
A division of NTC/Contemporary Publishing Group, Inc.
4255 West Touhy Avenue, Lincolnwood (Chicago), Illinois 60646-1975 U.S.A.
Copyright © 1999 by NTC/Contemporary Publishing Group, Inc.
Printed in the United States of America
International Standard Book Number: 0-8442-4541-0

98 99 00 01 02 03 QP 19 18 17 16 15 14 13 12 11 10 9 8 7 6 5 4 3 2 1

To Tim, Brian, and B.J.

Contents

Acknowledgments

Thanks to the Latinos and Latinas who shared with me their passion for their careers, and to the people who gave me their unique perspective on the workplace issues Latinos face. I also wish to express my gratitude to Patricia Lara Garza, Mariita Conley, Octavio Mateo, Anne Ladky, Karen Allen, and Joan Smith for their invaluable insight.

Thanks also to my parents, Oscar and Adela Kenig, for their unfailing belief in me, and to my husband, Tim Mazzaferri, without whose encouragement I could not have become a writer. Last but not least, I want to thank my son, Brian, for the nourishing love and support he gave me throughout my career.

Introduction

As the Jobs and Career columnist for *¡Exito!*, the Spanish-language newspaper published by the *Chicago Tribune*, I often meet other Latinos who are interested in hearing my opinion about a wide range of work-related issues. They want to know in what fields do Latinos have a competitive advantage...or, how Latinos should prepare for tomorrow's labor market. But beyond those general questions, some young Latino professionals also are looking for tips on practical ways to navigate the corporate world—from their unique perspective. Questions range from how to deal with office politics tainted by unfair stereotypes to advice on how to carve a career path without losing our Latino identity.

Over the years, I have covered many of those topics in my columns. During the writing process, I interviewed career experts, human resources specialists, professors, sociologists, heads of professional associations, Latinos who love their jobs, and people who have earned the right to be quoted because they have spent most of their adult life working in corporate America. Always, I choose interview subjects for their unique ideas or for a particular perspective that provides suggestions Latinos can apply easily and immediately to the workplace.

But what I couldn't do, until now, was to point to a source where all that collective wisdom had been gathered—a tool that could help Latinos to choose, shape, or change a career, using the best current options and proven strategies to succeed.

I wrote this book at the urging of several Latinos who felt it was badly needed. But it didn't take much convincing. Demographics show that Latinos are the fastest-growing minority in the United States and are expected to outnumber African Americans by the year 2015. Higher birth rates, continued immigration, and a younger age average in the Latino population explain why we are entering the labor market at faster rates than the non-Latino population, whose growth has slowed down considerably since the end of the baby boom.

Because Latinos lacked educational opportunities, many in our younger generations have not been exposed to professional role models. In many families, blue collar work has been the norm. While the young Latino university graduate is armed with strong values, he or she still has to navigate—and learn to succeed in—a vastly different world from the one in which our parents grew up.

In this new world, technological advances have blurred international borders, offering the same instant access to information around the globe. Today, competitiveness drives business decisions and the driving force is change. Only those who embrace change as an opportunity for growth will succeed. But Latinos already have much of what it takes to thrive in a fluctuating environment. This book will help them identify and utilize those values and strengths which best match the skills required in today's and tomorrow's labor market.

In a way, we Latinos have been preparing ourselves for the current state of change all our lives. If you attended American schools or worked in the United States, you had to negotiate between two cultures: home and school or home and job—and sometimes both. In a global economy, this ability to bridge contrasting cultural views is an invaluable skill. A second language, particularly Spanish, is icing on the cake.

Spanish is quickly becoming our nation's unofficial second language. According to the 1998 study of the U.S. Hispanic Market conducted by Strategy Research Corporation, 94 percent of adult Latinos living in the United States learned Spanish as their first language. As the survey also points out, people tend to be more receptive to marketing when approached in their native tongue. This explains the plethora of Spanish language and bilingual publications (such as *Latina Magazine*, and *People* and *Newsweek en Español*) which appeared in the late 1990s. Also, Latinos have become an important market segment in the United States with a buying power estimated to be more than $273 billion. Many of the jobs described in this book could probably be yours if, in addition to having the basic skills needed, you also speak Spanish.

Without a doubt, being bilingual increases employability. My own personal experience attests to that. Out of the ten jobs or consulting assignments I've had over the last twenty years, nine could be traced directly to the fact that I spoke English *and* Spanish. If you never learned to speak Spanish, I urge you to take courses now. It will not only open doors to new employment opportunities but it might also help you connect with your roots. When is the last time you had a good conversation with your *abuelita*? Granny could hold some wisdom that will never be passed on to you if you are English monolingual.

Read on for a thought-provoking look at how being a bilingual Latino can make a difference in your professional life.

Best Careers *for* Bilingual Latinos

Leveraging Your Language and Culture in Today's Job Market

Downsizing, restructuring, reengineering...these have been the buzzwords of the 1980s and 1990s. In their quest to remain competitive in a global economy—and to improve the bottom line—American corporations have been transforming themselves into lean institutions that can move forward at high speeds. That is why, at the turn of the twenty-first century, in spite of experiencing one of the lowest levels of unemployment in decades, American workers do not feel secure in their jobs.

With frequent and massive layoffs, job security is no longer a given. However, in a seller's market it takes less time to become employed once again—or to find quick, alternative solutions such as consulting, or temping for a while. This is especially true of people who have skills in high demand, often in fields related to high technology. For the rest of us, the key to rebounding quickly from a job loss is *employability*.

You are employable to the degree to which your skills and characteristics match the skills and characteristics employers need. These include the ability to solve problems, work well in teams, and take risks: all sought-after qualities that cut across all industries.

To remain employable, "you must constantly update your skills," advises Karen Allen, manager of the CareerWise program at Women Employed, a Chicago-based nonprofit that provides career development training to working women and also advocates on their behalf. "That way, if something happens in your current job, you are prepared to move on."

What this really means is that you're on your own, that you must become responsible for your own destiny. Your career must be portable and you should consider yourself a free agent or act like an entrepreneur whose business is his own career. In today's market, successful employees are those who get on the driver's seat of their professional lives.

The Road to Success

Sometimes it seems that the world is divided between sellers and buyers. At any given time, someone is either selling or buying a product or service. Looking for a job or exploring a career change is a very similar process. You, the candidate, must view yourself as a product that an employer *needs* to buy. And you must use some of the same tools marketers and advertisers rely on to sell their merchandise.

If you have ever sold anything, you know that the first rule is to know your product. In a job-search mode this means that you must invest in understanding yourself. In other words, you should analyze your strengths—those characteristics and skills that make you employable in the current market.

"At the supermarket we choose the brand of the things we want to buy," says Sara Headley, a Chicago-based consultant with more than twenty years of experience in sales. "Often, our choice is based on the packaging—what we see, as much as the taste, quality, and price. This is also true of a person: How do you look? What are your talents/skills? What are your likes and dislikes?"

Ultimately, only you can answer those questions and the ones that are listed below. For additional help, check the jobs section of a bookstore or library. Both have many self-discovery materials, some of which are listed in the resource sections of this book. The end result should be a list or lists that can provide you with a very special "self-portrait."

- What are you *passionate* about? Is this related to any of your hobbies? Sometimes, it is quite possible to turn an activity you love into a career. For example, an individual who truly enjoys gardening might consider becoming a landscape architect. Someone who is argumentative for the sheer pleasure of exercising the ability to use deductive reasoning might choose law or arbitration.

- What tasks/projects do you *enjoy* doing? Do you like dealing with figures or do you prefer activities related to reading or writing? The obvious deduction here would be that a numbers-type person might like the accounting or actuarial professions and the reader/writer would prefer an editorial occupation. However, some people enjoy a combination of these activities and only wish to have a predominance of the one they like most in their jobs.

- *How* do you like to accomplish your tasks? Do you prefer to work alone and need a quiet place to be productive? Or do you function better when you are surrounded by others with whom you can exchange ideas or work on joint projects?

- What paid or unpaid jobs did you do well in the past? Often, we overlook the things we do well simply because they seem effortless. For example, Carlos is the one who always volunteers to write or present his team's report to the rest of the department. Might it be that he does it because it is an easy task for him? Likewise, it might happen that Laura always becomes the treasurer of any organization she joins. Because the task seems so natural to her, it is possible that she may never think about the great deal of responsibility involved in being the treasurer—in addition to bookkeeping skills. She also may not realize that she volunteers to do this because she does it well and enjoys doing it.

- What things or issues are important to you, both at home and at work? Working and living in a friendly environment might be a significant factor for you. But being constantly challenged could be more to someone else's taste.

By now, a picture of your core personality traits and skills should be emerging. This is not only helpful in choosing a career but also in discovering what elements make you more employable. A key element can be found in your answer to the next question:

- What is unique about you? One possible reply could be that you can synthesize information quickly, or that you are a wizard with numbers, or have traveled a lot. But beyond that, you can add value to any company by virtue of being Latino.

Our Latino Strengths

Bilingual and bicultural Latinos can offer valuable assets to any firm wishing to compete in the global market. Following are some "sales" techniques you can use to describe such assets during job interviews or performance reviews. The italicized areas point to competencies today's employers expect.

"Once you know a second [language and] culture, it is considered easier to learn additional languages and understand other cultures," explains Victor Arias, executive vice president and managing director of DHR International, an executive search firm based in Irving, Texas. "In discussions with my clients, I find that many more are looking for multicultural employees."

"Bilingual and bicultural people see things from a different angle," adds Octavio Mateo, human relations manager for Citicorp in Fort Lauderdale, Florida, where his job is to provide support to all Latin American countries as well as those in the Caribbean. "It usually means that *you use different frames of reference* so you are better able to be an *analytical thinker*."

As the work force becomes more diverse, "those Latinos who are acculturated can provide a unique service to their employers," says Mariita Conley, of Conley, Arosemena & Associates, a Chicago-based firm that offers multicultural customer service and leadership training to large corporations. "They can help smooth [and speed up] the transition for those Latinos who are just coming in."

To measure your own employability, here are some additional qualities employers want. Many of them are natural to the Latino culture. If they are not a part of your skill set, they can be learned and practiced. Community colleges, professional organizations, and trade associations (hopefully in your field of interest) usually offer workshops on these topics. If you are currently employed, find out if your company provides this type of training or if they are willing to pay for you to obtain it elsewhere.

- Effective written and oral communication skills. In a fast-paced, bottom-line driven environment, you must be able to get your point across—whether through a memo or in person—quickly and effectively. There is no room for poor grammar, misspellings, or muddled thoughts. If you have trouble in this area, take a course. As executive recruiter Arias points out, "The first impression is what comes out of your mouth."

- Strong presentation skills. Today's employees must be able to present and/or defend an idea or project to groups of all sizes. If you are uncomfortable speaking in front of an audience, take a course and practice as much as possible—perhaps outside of work as a volunteer for a nonprofit organization. Your presentations will be stronger if you speak clearly, project self-confidence, and are able to get your point across.

- Flexibility and adaptability. Those of us who are immigrants have dealt with change before…a change of country, culture, and language, even a change of friends. If we were flexible enough to adapt to that new world, we can deal with change at work. Our strong *interpersonal skills* always carry us through times of ambiguity.

- Problem-solving capability or an orientation to getting results. In some of our families, problems are resolved by consensus. In others, they are resolved only by the head of the household. "Many Latinos come from cultures that do not reward individual achievement or initiative," says Conley. "When they have a problem, they go to an authority figure."

Others are completely at ease with the responsibility of solving problems. "If we have to get some work done, and need to go outside of our department, we use our networks and assemble a team," relates Gabriel Najera, an engineer and faculty member of the Amoco Management Learning Center in suburban Chicago. Fortunately, problem-solving skills are easy to teach and learn. If you are in the first group, take a course.

- Team-player mentality. "Latinos are adept at building relationships, we are natural networkers," says Najera. "We can use our networks to assemble teams, or to connect someone with a person who can help them solve a problem." In part, such a skill comes from our concept of family, which always includes all of our relatives and, very often, friends and the broader community. "All of us have one foot in the corporate world and the other in the community," Arias concurs. When anyone in our network needs help, *we know how to build consensus*. "It stems from the cooperative nature of our culture, in which decisions are largely made as a group," adds Conley.

- Computer literacy. In this day and age, even truck drivers rely on computers to measure load weights and arrange schedules. If you have managed to stay away from these useful machines so far, you will have no choice but to learn how to use them. If you are already comfortable working with a computer, learn how to use a new program or software package. The more skills you acquire, the more marketable you become.

- Loyalty to the job but not necessarily to the employer. While loyalty is one of our greatest assets, the kind of loyalty our parents gave to one or two employers over the course of their entire lives is a thing of the past. Employers now value candidates with broader experience, one which may include several companies, sometimes in different industries. They want candidates who are willing to commit themselves to doing the best possible job. According to Arias, that should be easy to do. "Latinos are much more passionate than other people," he says. "We do our job *con ganas* [with enthusiasm] and we are hard workers."

- Proper training and education in your particular field, along with the technical skills required to perform the job.

Of Special Interest to Latinas

At a workshop dealing with women in management, an Avon Products executive stated that Latinas are natural leaders. Here are the reasons she gave.

- We have the right traits. We are nurturing souls who look out for the needs of others. This is a strong motivator and it increases productivity.

- We have a strong work ethic and are willing to work hard. Both of these characteristics are needed to prevail in a changing labor market.

- Sociability. We value relationships and really know how to network—a skill recognized as a key ingredient of a successful career strategy.

Marketing Your Strengths

Once you have identified your strengths, you will want to apply them to your resume, and use them when you network, during informational or job interviews, salary negotiations, or performance reviews. But before you take that step, make sure that you are able to describe your strengths—both orally and in writing—in the best possible light and to your greatest advantage.

Sometimes this might entail dealing with self-imposed barriers that prevent you from showing your best side and letting your achievements shine.

"Generally, women [and minorities] are not comfortable promoting themselves," says Joan Smith, former career development director at Women Employed. "We have been taught to be humble, and to take a back seat. This makes it difficult to boldly talk about our accomplishments."

The cure for being afraid to toot your own horn, according to Smith, is to practice. "Find a safe environment where you can talk about the things you do well. Do this informally with friends and family and ask them to give you feedback. Sometimes you will say everything right but end up undoing it all because of your body language."

Once you are comfortable recognizing your accomplishments, figure out how to describe them in business language. As an example, Smith cites a woman who can manage a home effectively. Instead of using those words during a job interview or in her resume, she would say something like "I'm able to manage multiple priorities," or "I have extensive experience with crisis intervention."

Sales expert Sara Headley recommends that you focus on key skills such as *working well under pressure*, or *having the tendency to work methodically*, or *being a team player*. "Don't bother with things like you have a good sense of humor; it doesn't matter," she explains. "Likewise, if they ask you to name your unique selling points, don't waste time saying that you are patient or kind. What matters, for example, is whether or not you have a team mentality or can handle authority." It is important to know which things you can do well and which things you can't do. From that knowledge you can derive self-confidence.

Applying Your Research to the Tools of the Trade

What you discover through this process—along with the things you have always known—about yourself, can be applied to the job hunter's "tools of the trade." These include networking, job fairs, informational and job interviews, and resumes. The following sections will offer examples to guide you through some of these applications.

Your Particular Purpose

According to Joan Smith, the first step is to set objectives. Your purpose in seeking information determines the type of questions you will ask when you network or conduct informational interviews. As well, it will help you identify those individuals who might have the answers. For example, if you are looking for a job and know the kind of job you want, you may need to obtain the names of companies, the names of people in key companies, the organizations you should join, and the trade publications you should read. If, on the other hand, you are changing careers, you might want to know what skills, education, or prior experience are needed in the new field. As well, you will want to get feedback on the extent to which your background is a good fit.

However, Smith points out that "Most people fail in this process either because they didn't prepare their questions or because they asked the wrong person."

As an example, she cites a person who is potentially interested in working in the membership services department of an organization. "If she wants to know what 'a day in the life' of that department is like, she should ask the membership services coordinator," Smith explains. "If she wants to know what skills are needed to get that position, she should ask the coordinator's boss. And, if she wants to know about the trends in that particular field, she might ask the executive director."

Your Personal Script

Once you have clear objectives, it is a good idea to develop a brief statement describing who you are and what makes you unique. Much like those phrases the media calls sound bites, what you say needs to be meaningful, and communicate enough information about you to stand alone. Notice how this works in the following example, once a career changer couples his or her objectives with a personal script in a *networking situation*:

> "I am a highly effective and completely bilingual office manager and I'm looking for opportunities to use my skills in the health care field. Do you know any health care administrator I might talk with to find out more about the jobs in clinics, hospitals, or doctors' offices? Or do you know of any health-related institutions I could explore?"

In a similar setting, someone ready for a job change could say something like this instead:

> "I am an extremely resourceful and completely bilingual people motivator and I'm looking for opportunities to use my expertise in meeting planning. Do you know of any organizations or businesses that serve the Spanish-speaking community and might want to host an event this year?"

Depending on the ultimate goal, both of those personal script/objective combinations also can work at *job fairs*. Rather than simply handing over a resume, one can shake the company representative's hand, look him or her in the eye, and say one's piece. In a situation where company representatives may receive hundreds of resumes and talk to as many people in one day, this technique is much more effective. It is likely to open up the dialogue and leave a lasting impression of you and your resume.

When conducting an *informational interview* (which is done only for the purpose of obtaining information—not to get a job) there is more time to ask questions. The key, however, is to remain focused on the objectives.

Women Employed recommends establishing a link with the contact person ("so-and-so suggested that I call you"), and then putting your request for information into context, as in the following example:

> "My employer, Company Blue, announced massive layoffs that will take place over the next several months."

Then you can bridge into the questions you need to ask.

> "I am an exceedingly proficient bilingual researcher with five years of experience in applied chemical research and would like to use my skills in the international arena. Do you know with whom I might talk about the possibility of doing a tour of duty in a Latin American manufacturing company?"

These brief personal descriptions and requests for information also can be applied to resumes. In his book *Top Secret Resumes and Cover Letters* (Dearborn Publishing, 1995), author Steven Provenzano says that resumes should be future-oriented and recommends that you begin this document with a stated objective. If the above chemist were to follow Provenzano's advice, this is how his objective would read:

> To do applied chemical research in a multinational manufacturing concern where I can apply my knowledge of the Latino culture and utilize the Spanish language.

He would then back up his objective, in a later section of the resume, with a statement along these lines:

> More than ten years of experience in the development and production of synthetic glues, including total responsibility over Latin American projects. Developed RPG Glue, a fast-drying compound currently being applied to furniture manufacturing in Costa Rica.

Know Your Customer

At this point, you can move the sales process to the next level: Know your customer. Before you interview for a job with any company, find out what product it makes or sells. Also, how long they have been in business, if the work is fast or slow-paced, old-fashioned, or at the cutting edge of technological discoveries, and if people work there for three years or thirty. You can get all this information from the company's annual report, by checking periodicals for past articles about the company, or talking to current or past employees.

Headley adds that this information, coupled with your self-knowledge, will allow you to decide beforehand whether or not to interview with a company. "While sometimes it is not possible to find out these things before the interview, remember that the company does not want to hire someone who will not be happy working there." Would *you* want to be dissatisfied with your job?

Before or during the interview, make sure that your customer (a.k.a. the potential employer) really needs someone with your skill set and experience. Just as you wouldn't try to sell baby clothes to a pharmacist, there is no point in marketing your bilingualism to a company that never deals with Spanish-speaking customers or employees. If there is no match, you might as well redirect your search.

When going for the sale, think about it as a final sale—no refunds, no exchanges. Ask yourself "am I really going to like it here?" If you quit within three months you will have wasted your time and the company's, which translates into a lot of money.

Headley feels that if you make your job decision this way, it will come from the right place and will become a win-win situation for both you and the employer.

- Go for the close (ask for the sale). "When the interview is done, don't say 'gee, I'd like to work here'," warns Headley. "Instead, say 'this sounds wonderful, I would really like the job.' This allows the employer to make a purchasing decision. Only when that has been done can you begin negotiating the terms—particularly about the salary they may offer, or the one you may accept."

- Follow up. This is just as important for the seller as it is for the buyer. Send a thank-you letter suggesting the next step needed to "close the deal."

In Summary

- Think of yourself as a product you want to sell and a customer needs to buy.

- Know your product (identify your strengths, including those that make you unique because you are Latino, and learn to describe them in business language).

- Prepare your personal script and apply it to networking sessions, informational interviews, and to your resume (but remember to be brief and unique).

- Know your customer. Research potential employers before even approaching them. Do they need you or your skills? Is there a good match?

- Go for the close.

Resources

Marketing Yourself by Dorothy Leeds (New York: HarperCollins, 1991).

Getting Hired in the 90's by Vicki Spina (Chicago: Dearborn Financial Publishing, 1995).

When *You* Are the Diversity at Work

Even though corporate America is increasingly diverse, it is not unusual for us to be the only Latinos or minority members of a team or department—or one of the very few in the higher managerial ranks. When that is the case, we tend to feel isolated. Somehow, it seems easier to emphasize our differences than to look for and acknowledge what we have in common with people of the dominant culture.

It is an unhappy situation. And it is counterproductive. How can you focus on the work that needs to be done under such circumstances? How do you go about finding allies? Or figure out the unwritten codes and rules that govern that particular environment? And how can you follow these rules without losing your cultural identity?

It has to start with you. No one will approach you if you hide behind your desk or look away. And, as long as you behave that way, you may keep your cultural identity intact but will remain isolated and in a dead-end position.

In *The Colorblind Career* by Ollie Stevenson with Dana Huebler, the authors describe today's mainstream business culture as a "mind-set" which encompasses the behaviors, attitudes, and values of the majority of its members (still white males, primarily). While in time you may be able to change parts or all of that mindset, if you want to function in the current business environment now, you must first adhere to the accepted rules.

No one is suggesting that you stop being who you are. But there must be some bending if you wish to cultivate a successful career. The following strategies, some of which were given to me by a now retired McDonald's executive whose specialty was human resources, can help you reduce your cultural isolation without giving up your values.

- Ask questions. It will give you a chance to network, and it will begin to fill in the information blanks you have about the place.

- Identify potential helpers or mentors (in the same way you would try to decide which cousin could help you with one thing or another). Find out who knows what about which project or department, and who holds the power.

- Find out the company's goals and align yourself with them. It shows initiative and gives you the right focus. If their goal is to increase sales in an ethnic neighborhood, why not suggest one? You can facilitate the process through your contacts in the Latino communities you know.

- Volunteer to work on projects which help the company grow—especially those which mesh with your values (food pantries? medical assistance?). This will give you visibility, and practice at working with teams.

- Help the company recruit more Latinos; it will reduce your isolation. Perhaps you know someone who would be a good fit.

- Help the company do more business with Latinos. If you work for a bank, for example, you could connect someone in the lending department with an uncle who owns a *bodega* (grocery store).

Understanding Stereotypes

Being the only (or one of the few) Latino(s) in a particular business setting can make us keenly aware of behaviors which appear to be based on stereotypical notions about "our people." While that is a painful situation, we are not the only victims. For every group of people, our society seems to have a set of destructive beliefs. And, whether we like it or not, we ourselves have bought into one stereotype or another at some point in time—or at least thought that a portion of each must be true. Consider the following examples and ask yourself if you ever assumed that any of these statements were true:

- Women can't be leaders. If they are promoted, it must be because they slept their way to the top.
- If a woman is authoritative, she's a bitch.
- All [Blacks/Latinos/Asians] are submissive.
- Men are rational beings. They take charge and always know what to do.

These beliefs separate and confuse people. For example, if one subscribes to the theory that all minorities are submissive, then the image of a minority male in a position of authority becomes incongruous.

Where do these beliefs originate? Sociologists say that *at least a part* of each stereotype, *was true of at least one person* in a particular group at some point in time. For example, it is entirely possible that, some time in the past, an individual noticed that a Latino (or maybe even two) was behaving in a submissive manner. The trouble is, that person communicated his belief to others and, soon enough, it was extended to *all* Latinos.

In the book *Working Together*, authors George Simons and Amy Zuckerman say that our minds have what psychologists call "confirmation bias." In other words, if we think certain groups of people are lazy, we will always notice when *they*—but not others—do something that confirms such an assumption (for example, they are late). The "halo effect," on the other hand, leads us to believe if a person is good—or not good—at something (such as operating machines), the same will be true of something else (i.e., reading).

Once the confirmation bias takes hold, what may have been a generalization becomes a stereotype—attributing one personality to an entire group. People who believe the stereotypes are closed to new information and usually respond to the stereotyped group with negative treatment.

It is difficult, but not impossible, to change some of the behaviors that stem from those beliefs. If you allow the resulting feelings to fester, they can have a devastating effect on your self-esteem and reduce your productivity at work.

Overcoming Stereotypes

The key to overcoming stereotypes—ours and theirs—is to get to know one another so we can debunk those beliefs. However, you must recognize that you only control what *you* do or say—never someone else's behavior.

The change starts with you. Here are some tips that can help defuse or overcome the effects of stereotypes.

- Demonstrate that the myth does not apply to you. For example, if people assume you are submissive, show them that you are not. Walk with your head high, make eye contact, offer a firm handshake, take advantage of every opportunity to develop and showcase your leadership abilities. Or, if co-workers ignore your contributions, point them out as often as is appropriate.

- Introduce yourself to others. "People like to work with you when they feel comfortable with you," says Amoco's Gabriel

Najera. "Once they get to know you and see that your work is good, it is up to you to show them that you are not unique…that you are not the only Mexican [or Puerto Rican/Guatemalan, etc.] whose work is good."

- However, the above does not mean that you should become the representative or spokesperson for all other Latinos at your place of employment. Avoid falling into the trap of having to explain to *those people* how *we Latinos* do one thing or another. "How can you do that when you can't possibly know everyone of your same race and gender?" asks Bernita Berry, a sociologist and associate professor at Prairie View A & M University in Prairie View, Texas. "Besides, that topic of conversation has nothing to do with work," she continues. "If someone wants to know about 'your people,' refocus their attention and ask questions to help you learn more about the position above yours." For example, "What does it take to become the vice president of this company?"

- Find a co-worker from a different cultural background and learn about each other's culture.

- Get used to keeping track of your work-related accomplishments in writing—and share this document with your boss and/or co-workers whenever it is appropriate (for example, when bidding for a team leadership position or a promotion). "This will give others a chance to learn about your skills and become more familiar with you," explains Pat Yauch, president of Work Transitions Partners, Inc., a consulting firm in suburban Chicago. "Because this document is based on fact, it is not a bragging mechanism."

- If you truly think you are the victim of discrimination, find out if others in the company (such as women, or other minorities, etc.) feel discriminated against as well. But even if you are the only one, there are legal steps you can take. Check with the EEOC office closest to you.

Avoiding Pitfalls

In any workplace, there are certain stereotyping pitfalls that you should try to avoid at all costs. As a rule, avoid:

- making quick judgments about what someone said or did. Ask for clarification before you jump to conclusions. Poor communication is the most common problem in multicultural organizations. If, for example, you do not get a glowing performance review, don't rush to the conclusion that this has to do with the race or gender of your evaluator, which is different from yours. Look at the comments objectively and ask questions about what is being said. Otherwise, you add your own stereotypes to the equation.

- spending your time *exclusively* with the majority groups, or with the other Latinos who work in your company. "Both extremes are counterproductive because they are barriers to cooperative relations in the workplace," explains Professor Berry. Talking with the other Latinos does not automatically mean that you are planning a coup to overtake the company. By the same token, talking to people in other ethnic groups does not mean you are forgetting your own roots. Treat everyone with the same respect, courtesy, and friendliness.

- speaking Spanish in front of others who do not understand the language. Even if you are not talking about them, this gives the impression that you are, and it is disrespectful. It is also an inappropriate behavior in the workplace.

- putting others down, telling ethnic jokes, disrespecting the opinions of others. If someone else tells offensive jokes in your presence, you simply state that you do not appreciate hearing that and walk away. "But you must do it *when* it happens, and in front of the others who also heard the joke" warns Berry. "It loses effectiveness if you point out the problem later when both of you are alone."

Gender: the Additional Barrier

By virtue of being women, working Latinas face additional barriers, many of which stem from stereotypes that can affect their work performance.

"My boss triple checks everything I turn in," complains Luisa Torres (not her real name). "He doesn't do that with the reports the men turn in. It makes me feel so incompetent."

Other Latinas report lack of support on the part of their husbands (even though they work out of necessity), and still others believe they haven't advanced in their careers solely because they are women. The glass ceiling still exists. In fact, a woman executive recently mentioned that it should be called the plastic ceiling. "At least glass can break," she mused.

Another difficulty Latinas face has to do with socialization. "We are taught that the family comes first and the career second," says Patricia Lara Garza, a consultant who specializes in issues of diversity and the workplace. "You have to be an outstanding mother even if you achieve great things at work. But the corporate sector demands great sacrifices that affect the family—long hours, travel…that's when many Latinas opt out of the fast track."

Getting Along

Office politics often complicate an already delicate multicultural situation—yet they can't be avoided.

"Most people have been hurt by office politics so they don't believe there is a positive aspect to them," says Yauch. "But the essence of office politics is the competition for few available resources. These are actually techniques used to gain power."

Power is the capacity to accomplish things through others. Do you have such power, even if you are not in a management position? Yauch believes it is entirely possible to be powerful if you aren't greedy about it—that is, you share your power when necessary—and learn to engage in win-win situations.

For example, you can suggest a collaborative relationship with a co-worker, who is preferably a member of another culture, be it dominant or minority. This could take the shape of projects where both of you can shine, such as joint presentations, or events you plan together. These opportunities promote multicultural interaction and can move your career forward in a positive way.

Using Politics to Your Advantage

To use office politics to your advantage, try some of Yauch's tips:

- Do a little soul-searching. How do you feel about your standing in the company? Is there something you wish to improve? What stories do people tell about you?

  "These stories will determine the influence you have in an organization," Yauch explains.

  If you think about the stories people tell about you, you will see that, very often, they can be traced directly to something you said in the past. The next time you speak to a co-worker about how challenging a given project was for you (or how badly you feel about something you did or said) remember that you are providing him or her with ammunition. Such information can become a killer bullet if it resurfaces in the wrong context and at the wrong time.

  Lesson: Never share your difficulties about work-related matters with anyone at work—especially not your boss.

- Make a list of the people in your company, and rank them according to the influence they have on your ability to do your job. These individuals can be bosses, colleagues, secretaries, or maintenance people. Treat each one of them with respect. Someday they may do something to ease your job: fix the copy machine in a hurry, let you talk to the boss first, or perhaps be more careful with your presentation materials.

- Review the above list and separate the "partners" and "allies" from the "detractors." You will want to negotiate a way to win the support of the latter group.

In Summary

- If you are the only, or one of the few, Latinos in your department or company, take the first step and talk to others to learn the rules of the game and to feel less isolated.

- When it comes to stereotypes, remember that you can only control your own behavior. Redirect all racial and ethnic conversations toward topics that have to do with the work you must perform.

- Treat everyone with the same respect, courtesy, and friendliness.

- Recognize office politics for what it is: a competition for power. Engage only in win-win situations, and don't tell stories that may turn into ammunition against you later.

Resources

The Colorblind Career: What Every African American, Hispanic American and Asian American Needs to Know to Succeed in Today's Tough Job Market by Ollie Stevenson with Dana Huebler, (Peterson's Guides, 1997).

Latino Success: Insights from 100 of America's Most Powerful Latino Business Professionals by Augusto Failde and William Doyle (Simon and Schuster, 1997).

Working Together: Succeeding in a Multicultural Organization by George Simons with Amy Zuckerman (Crisp Publications, Inc., 1994).

Getting What You Need to Succeed

No matter what career you choose, you are more likely to be happy at work if your personal values agree with the professional values your company espouses. For example, if you are someone who values time with your family but your company does not offer flex-time options, eventually you could become resentful. Sooner or later, you'll want to make a change.

"Values are the essence of who we are," observes Linda Bruemmer, vice president of Right/Jannotta Bray, a career counseling firm based in Northbrook, Illinois. "They are the force that guides our decisions."

But when a conflict of values signals that it is time to make a change, your decision may not mean getting a new job. Sometimes we may decide that we can exercise our values outside of our jobs, perhaps through volunteering efforts. Other times we can take steps to modify our current environment and increase the degree of satisfaction with our jobs. In the family-time example above, the person could survey the company to see how many other employees would be interested in having flexible hours. Armed with data, he or she could meet with a supervisor to find out if management is even willing to discuss the possibility of offering such a benefit, or if a telecommuting arrangement can be made.

Before you prepare to look for a job, or consider making a career change, you must be clear about your own values. Think about them and make a list. It could include faith, family, helpfulness, achievement, adventure, cooperation, or any other value you deem important.

But Bruemmer says that it is not enough to voice your values. She proposes that you also examine your past actions and decisions to check your list against reality. "We demonstrate our values by our behaviors and our choices."

Only those values that you have exercised are the ones that should remain on your list. Use them as a guide when you research potential employers, particularly during informational and job interviews.

Networking

Social networking skills are much like professional networking skills, and are at least as important.

However, some of us have trouble getting started, while others do not network effectively. This section offers some solutions.

Eliminate Barriers

When it comes to networking, some of us cannot get beyond the people we already know. Once we have blanketed our inner circle, we seem to hit a wall. Sometimes, this happens because we are reluctant to ask for help, believing perhaps we are supposed to know how to handle everything on our own. Other times, there may be a fear of rejection. One may wonder, "Why would anyone want to help me?" Occasionally, it is because we are not sure of what to say or how to say it. Are we comfortable talking about ourselves? Can we describe our own accomplishments?

By definition, networking is essentially a conversation during which you ask a series of questions in search of specific information that can yield other contacts. The type of questions you ask depends on your objectives. The clearer you are about the information you need, the easier it becomes to obtain it and the more comfortable you feel about asking. Preparation is the key factor in helping you overcome psychological barriers.

Before you attend any networking event, prepare yourself. Define your goals, develop your questions, and create a personal script which describes you and your accomplishments succinctly. (See "Applying Your Research to the Tools of the Trade" in Chapter 1.)

"Your questions need to be very focused and targeted," suggests Women Employed's Karen Allen. You might ask, for example, if the person knows one or two individuals with experience in your field of interest. Could you contact them to conduct informational interviews and use this person's name as a referral? Other questions include: "Which are the most important companies in this field? What trade journals do you recommend I read to keep up with this industry's trends?"

"Above all, practice with as many people as possible, especially with others who are currently working," says Allen. Their feedback can be very helpful, and you will greatly increase your comfort level.

Effective Networking

While some Latinos cannot get beyond their immediate circle of friends and family, there are others among us who never know when to stop. These individuals are such social beings, and like to have so much fun, that even though they collect many business cards, they leave the event having gathered very little useful information.

This syndrome also can be avoided with preparation. In addition to developing your questions and personal script, decide beforehand how many people you will target at the networking event. In most cases, two or three sources of information are sufficient—provided they yield the desired results. The truth is that, if we gather fifteen to twenty cards, most of us will rarely have the time to call so many people.

Once you obtain the information you need, you can really enjoy the rest of the event without the pressure to keep "working the room" with ulterior motives.

How Others Can Help You

Latinos who were raised in the context of an extended family, which often included friends, find much resonance in the mentoring concept. Did you not have an uncle or aunt, an older cousin, a *padrino*, who helped you through rough times? Or who gave you a push when you needed it most? Most of us gratefully remember an occasion like that.

It is not such a leap, then, to transfer this idea to the business world. Say you landed a job and need to learn the unwritten behavior rules of the company. Or you want to move up the career ladder but are not sure which path is more valued in that company. Or you were assigned to a project that requires some skills you do not have. Whom do you turn to for help? You would probably talk to someone who has been through some similar experiences and can provide you with a new perspective. Usually this helper is a mentor.

Strength in Numbers

Just as one particular uncle couldn't possibly know it all, one mentor no longer suffices. In her book *Success 2000* futurist Vicki Spina proposes that everyone form their own "advisory board." This is a group of people you select, on the basis of an established relationship of mutual respect, who can give you advice on different areas of expertise. Need to do something too technical for your skills? One of your members should be able to help.

Having several mentors also makes sense in today's business climate where time is precious and everyone's schedule is overcrowded. If you approach people to request that they be your mentor, they may turn you down simply because it feels like and is a big commitment. But if you develop relationships with people you admire, and obtain their guidance through targeted meetings within a limited period of time, you don't even have to tell them that you consider them mentors. You become two professionals *exchanging* information. (You should always make it a point to be of help to this person, lest this develop into a one-way relationship.)

Identifying Mentors

Before you even approach a potential mentor, Spina suggests that you define your objectives. Typical business examples are for recommendations for a particular presentation or ideas to increase your visibility. This will make it easier to identify the people who can help you.

Ideally, you should seek mentors outside of your department or company. They can provide you with a different perspective, devoid of office politics and personal competition. It is perfectly acceptable to have a mentor of the opposite sex. Linda Garza Connor, an engineer who works for T.U. Electric in Dallas, did just that. Through a program designed to help women secure mentors, created by the Minnesota-based Menttium Corporation, Garza Connor was matched with a male engineer who works for Pizza Hut and was born in Egypt. "He is a fascinating, wonderful person to work with," she says. "And he has a very broad outlook because he has traveled all over the world. I'm an electrical engineer and he has a doctorate in chemical engineering. That gave us the foundation to start the relationship."

Professional organizations also are a good source of mentors. Usually, senior members or industry experts offer seminars or presentations aimed at developing your career. One such organization is the Hispanic Alliance for Career Enhancement (HACE) in Chicago. In addition to an annual conference and Career Expo for Latino professionals, they maintain a job bank, offer "how to" workshops, and secure scholarships for Latino students.

A Word of Caution

Once you have selected your mentors and established relationships with them, always weigh their advice against your own instincts and experience. Unfortunately, many of us have been burned by the wrong advice. A high school counselor told me, when I was a recent immigrant, not to apply for financial aid for my freshman year in college. I still wonder, "What was he thinking?" My friend was accepted to several good colleges and her parents advised her to choose the one closest to home. She attended that school even though it was the least prestigious. (Her parents had no experience in that regard because no one in the family had attended college before.) I am sure you have some tales of your own. If your gut tells you that the advice you received is not for you, ask your mentor why he thought that was the best route. Then test that notion by asking someone else's opinion.

Last, but not least, consider becoming a mentor to someone younger. Our youth need role models who can encourage them to stay in school. Once you get to know them, you will reap many benefits as well.

Leadership Versus Management

Not so long ago, moving up the career ladder meant taking the traditional route toward management. However, many layers of middle management have disappeared in the wake of mergers, restructuring, and downsizing. Today's business environment demands teamwork and leaders.

Joe Castillo, a senior executive with the Xerox Corporation, believes there is a real difference between management and leadership. At an event sponsored by Chicago's HACE, he said that you *can* be a manager and a leader at the same time. The difference between the two is that *leaders have vision*. As an example he cited President Kennedy, whose vision in the early sixties was to put a man on the moon by the end of the decade. It happened in 1969.

Do you have a vision? A personal mission? Where do you want to be in two years, five years, or ten years? While it is difficult to set long-term goals in a fluctuating business environment, having a purpose in life allows you to remain focused. Even if job or life situations change suddenly, you will always know where you are going.

Some people's vision may be to make a difference in somebody else's life. For others, it may be to invent a helpful machine, design or build a building, write a novel, or feel challenged at work. What all these examples have in common is that you can continue working toward those goals regardless of your job situation. If you make the commitment to achieve your mission, it becomes your center—the point to which you will return every time you need to shift gears.

Leading by Example

Because your mission is grounded in your values, it is likely to be reflected in everything you do, from the way you relate to your peers to the choices you make. When you begin to inspire others, you have become a leader. This can happen in your personal life (in a church committee, for example) or in the professional arena, whether you are in charge of a team or only one of its participants.

At work you are a good team leader, for example, if you take the time to communicate the company's vision (which is hopefully aligned with yours) to members of the team. Only then are they able to understand what is expected of them in the context of where they are going. You also show leadership when you make decisions based on facts rather than emotions, and can move your team in the direction that points to the company's desired outcomes.

Your attitude plays a big role in this process. When you generate enthusiasm, your team members may feel inclined to imitate it. "If you always walk with your head down, who will want to follow you?" Castillo asked.

New Expectations for Leaders

Having said all that, you should know that the future will require a whole new set of skills for leaders. "The game has changed," explains Michael Wynne, president of International Management

Consulting Associates in Naperville, Illinois. "We are moving away from the old, very structured approach where you had to dot all the i's and cross all the t's. We don't have time to do things that way anymore because the flood of information we receive comes to us too quickly."

That is why the effective leader will be someone who "develops the mental structure needed to perceive the heart of an issue and make a decision—very much like doctors, who are trained to recognize patterns, make a diagnosis," he adds.

For that reason, Wynne maintains that, among other things, tomorrow's leaders will need to give precedence to focus over order; awareness over certainty; results over process; fast, good decisions over slow, perfect decisions; and doing the right thing over doing things right.

Xerox Corporation's Castillo has a list of needed skills which includes a high standard of personal ethics, high energy, and an ability to set priorities. Other important qualities include the ability to be courageous, hard-working, goal-oriented, unorthodox, and creative.

Practice behaving that way at work and, soon enough, your leadership qualities will make you shine.

In Summary

- Regardless of the career you choose, or have chosen, make sure it agrees with your personal values. This is a key factor in achieving career satisfaction.

- On the road to success, take advantage of your innate qualities to network so you can get the best possible information about the next interview, the next job, a new career path, and the people you should meet.

- Identify several people, preferably outside of your department or company, and establish a quasi-mentoring relationship with each. (Don't tell them you want them to be your mentors; simply get together or talk only for very targeted reasons.)

Develop your leadership abilities by defining your own personal and professional visions. Dare to lead by example. Learn the rules of the new game so you can be ready for tomorrow's economy.

Resources

Organizations:

The Hispanic Alliance for Career Enhancement (HACE)
200 S. Michigan Avenue, Suite 1210
Chicago, IL 60604
(312) 435-0498
Links Hispanic professionals to public and private organizations.

National Hispanic Employee Association
2011 N. Shoreline Boulevard
M/S 954
Mountain View, CA 94043
(650) 933-6953

Menttium Corporation
8009 34th Avenue, Suite 1350
Bloomington, MN 55425
(612) 814-2600

Corporate mentoring program for women, with branches in several states.

Books:

Make Your Connections Count: The Six-Step System to Build Your Meganetwork by Melissa Giovagnoli. (Dearborn Trade, 1995).

Success 2000: Moving into the Millennium With Purpose, Power, and Prosperity by Vicki Spina. (John Wiley & Sons, 1997).

Best Careers for Bilingual Latinos

I f you are about to select your first career or are considering a change, this guide will help you survey a variety of fields. They were selected because of their expected long-term ability to provide continued employment, in light of labor market and demographic changes.

Because no one can predict the future, the trends described below should be used as a career exploration tool. Ultimately, the choices you make should be based on careful analysis of your skills and values, checked against those which are needed for those occupations. A passion for, or an intense interest in, the field also is important. It will make your work much more satisfying. In the 1980s, for example, many people rushed to get MBA degrees because individuals with such degrees were said to be in high demand. Later, many of them discovered that the business world was not their calling. Don't let that happen to you.

The Trends

According to the Bureau of Labor Statistics, between 1996 and 2006 employment will grow the fastest and increase the most in **professional specialty occupations**. The lion's share of that growth (nearly five million jobs) is expected among teachers, librarians, and counselors; computer, mathematical, and operations research occupations; and health assessment and treatment occupations. Engineering, also included in this occupational category, will add 244,000 jobs to the economy.

The second-fastest growth rate is expected in the category of **technicians** and **related support occupations**, a relatively small group that will contribute 940,000 jobs and includes health technicians and technologists; engineering and science technicians and technologists; and computer programmers and paralegals. In contrast, **marketing** and **sales occupations** will increase by 2.3 million workers, and **administrative support occupations**, including **clerical**, will grow by 1.8 million jobs. **Service occupations** will add 3.9 million jobs, nearly two-thirds of which are in the health, social, and business services industries.

Table 1 lists the fastest growing occupations, selected from the top thirty, which require at least some on-the-job training. Table 2 lists the occupations with the largest job growth, also selected from the top thirty and requiring at least some on-the-job training. The occupations that appear on both lists are the most promising.

A Reality Check

Some of these trends are already evident at the Hispanic Alliance for Career Enhancement in Chicago (HACE), where a job bank links Latino professionals with corporations.

"Corporations are now looking for candidates with a particular combination of skills," says José Gómez, the organization's executive director. "For example, they'll ask for someone with MIS

Table 1

Selected Fastest-Growing Occupations, 1996–2006

Occupation	Additional Jobs	Percent Change	Education/ Training Needed
Database administrators, computer support specialists, & all other computer scientists	249,000	118	Bachelor's degree
Computer engineers	235,000	109	Bachelor's degree
Systems analysts	520,000	103	Bachelor's degree
Physical & corrective therapy assistants & aides	66,000	79	Moderate-term on-the-job training
Medical assistants	166,000	74	Moderate-term on-the-job training
Desktop publishing specialists	22,000	74	Long-term on-the-job training
Physical therapists	81,000	71	Bachelor's degree
Paralegals	76,000	68	Associate's degree
Occupational therapists	38,000	66	Bachelor's degree
Teachers, special education	241,000	59	Bachelor's degree
Human services workers	98,000	55	Moderate-term on-the-job training
Health information technicians	44,000	51	Associate's degree
Speech-language pathologists & audiologists	44,000	51	Master's degree
Physician assistants	39,000	47	Bachelor's degree
Engineering, science & computer systems managers	155,000	45	Work experience plus bachelor's or graduate degree
Securities & financial services sales workers	10,0000	38	Bachelor's degree

Source: *Current Population Survey*, Bureau of Labor Statistics, U.S. Department of Labor

[management of information systems] and some management experience, or someone with MIS and marketing or an MBA. The Latino who has those skills can almost decide where to work and how much to earn."

Table 2
Selected Occupations with the Largest Job Growth, 1996–2006

Occupation	Additional Jobs	Percent Change	Education/ Training Needed
Systems analysts	520,000	103	Bachelor's degree
General managers & top executives	467,000	15	Work experience plus bachelor's or graduate degree
Registered nurses	411,000	21	Associate's degree
Salespersons, retail	408,000	10	Short-term on-the-job training
Teacher aides & educational assistants	370,000	38	Short-term on-the-job training
Teachers, secondary school	312,000	22	Bachelor's degree
Database administrators, computer support specialists, & all other computer scientists	249,000	118	Bachelor's degree
Marketing & sales workers, supervisors	246,000	11	Work experience in related occupation
Teachers, special education	241,000	59	Bachelor's degree
Computer engineers	235,000	109	Bachelor's degree
Social workers	188,000	32	Bachelor's degree
Food service & lodging managers	168,000	28	Work experience in related occupation
Medical assistants	166,000	74	Moderate-term on-the-job training

Source: *Current Population Survey,* Bureau of Labor Statistics, U.S. Department of Labor

Sallie Woods Gottof, who worked as the organization's recruitment team leader, explains that most corporations approach HACE for one of three reasons. "Normally, they call because they are looking to fill positions in the emerging [foreign] markets, the domestic Hispanic markets, or because of diversity issues."

While those search categories remain the same, HACE has seen a change in each over the years. Larger business-to-business companies are now interested in Latinos for their emerging markets. "They need bilingual people to sell, market, and distribute their products in Latin America," Woods Gottof adds.

But perhaps the biggest shift the organization has experienced has been in positions related to consumer products. "Whereas we used to get calls mostly from companies like Quaker Oats, we are now also getting requests from the financial services sector, with companies such as Dean Witter and Harris Bank."

Clearly, this points to a domestic Latino market for financial services, such as home and car loans, which reflects the increasing prosperity of our community. In some areas of the country, such as the Midwest, that market is largely untapped, offering excellent opportunities for both business and employment.

The Top Seven Fields for Bilingual Latinos

These fields were selected because they are expected to remain healthy in spite of recent or foreseen major changes, to endure based on population needs and behavioral trends, and to offer continued high demand for employees in general, and bilingual Latinos in particular.

They are:

Health Care

Financial Services

Technology

Sales and Marketing

Public Service

Professional Services

International Opportunities

Because each of these fields is broad in scope and encompasses numerous occupations, only some will be featured in detail in the corresponding chapters. Following is the selection criteria:

- The occupation is among—or closely related to—the fastest growing occupations or the occupations with the largest number of projected job openings between 1996 and 2006. (See Tables 1 and 2.)

- Being a bilingual Latino adds value to this occupation or represents a competitive advantage for job seekers.

- It offers room for professional growth.

- It has portability (the skills needed can transfer into other professions in the same field or to other industries).

> *A note about salaries*: Average or median annual earnings will be provided for each occupation. However, this factor was not included in the above criteria because, in general, people have different opinions as to what constitutes "a lot" or "not enough" money. In addition, some folks are willing to earn "little money," as long as they can do something they enjoy. For others, a high salary always comes first.

The information that appears in the following chapters is only a beginning. As you explore different occupations, be sure to conduct informational interviews or to job-shadow someone already working in that profession. Ask what they like most about their work. What keeps them excited? What parts of the job do they hate and why? Are there many Latinos in that occupation or would you be one of the pioneering few? What about career mobility? Salary expectations? Or anything which is important to you? What you see and hear during such sessions can save you time, money, and a lot of grief. It is very upsetting to reach your senior year in college and to realize, only then, that you hate the career you have picked. Or to have accepted a job and, after only five days, wish it were all a bad dream.

If you are reading these pages because you are a career changer, do some soul-searching first: What do you like about your current career? What elements of your current job do you wish to eliminate? And which do you want to keep? What values which are prevalent in the new field match yours? Are there some values in that field that you dislike? If so, can you live with them? It is not uncommon to see someone who outwardly has made a big change, yet the new field has many of the same elements this person hated in the old career. The way to avoid that situation is to be true to yourself, and to conduct as many informational interviews as possible before you attempt to shift gears.

Regardless of the occupation you choose, make a commitment to being a lifelong learner. This can mean attending workshops to update your skills, studying to attain a higher educational degree, or taking a course simply because you like the topic and it gives you something new to think about. When the next opportunity presents itself, whatever it may be, you will be ready to jump in or choose to turn away. It will have little, if anything, to do with luck.

Resources

Web sites

Some of the following *web sites* contain career and job hunting advice; others connect you directly with job listings in your field of interest. Some provide both.

> www.petersons.com—Peterson's Guides, Inc.
>
> www.JobWeb.com—National Association of Colleges and Employers.
>
> www.Saludos.com—*Saludos Hispanos* magazine.
>
> www.careercity.com (JobBank)—Adam's Media Corporation.
>
> www.careermosaic.com—Bernard Hodes Advertising.
>
> www.monster.com (Monster Board)—TMP Worldwide, Inc.

Books

What Color Is Your Parachute? by Richard Nelson Bolles (Ten Speed Press—get most recent volume. It is updated annually.)

The Best Companies for Minorities by Lawrence Otis Graham and Rosabeth Moss Kanter (Plume, 1993).

Health Care Careers

The aging of the baby boom generation and the fact that we are now living longer and surviving once-fatal diseases will increase the need for workers in the health care industry for years to come. According to the Bureau of Labor Statistics, more than half of the thirty fastest growing occupations have significant employment in the health sector, which is expected to increase more than twice as fast as the economy as a whole and add over three million jobs by 2006.

While there are many administrative occupations related to running clinics and hospitals (as one would run a corporation), most people in this field are primarily involved in diagnosing, treating, and preventing illnesses. Their jobs range from doctors and nurses to recreational therapists, who work in clinics, hospitals, doctors' offices, medical centers, hospices, and private homes. Bilingual health care workers are desperately needed in many of these occupations, especially those that require direct contact with patients, where language barriers interfere with treatment or service delivery. The need is most acute in urban areas with the largest concentrations of Latinos: Miami, New York, Los Angeles, San Antonio, and Chicago.

Intense competition within the industry, primarily because of the continued growth in the number of health maintenance organizations (HMOs), precipitated its own ongoing transformation. In terms of jobs with patient interaction, this has meant primarily a change of venue. Many medical procedures that used to be performed in hospitals are now taking place in outpatient facilities. And shorter hospital stays have created the need for follow-up home care.

The Jobs

Occupations in the health care sector are many and varied. This chapter will highlight some jobs that are ideal for bilingual Latinos, but will focus on those that meet the criteria described in Chapter 4. If you are interested in this field, take math and science courses and obtain paid or volunteer experience in the health care setting of your choice.

Figures in parenthesis reflect the projected number of workers that will be needed through the year 2006 due to growth and net replacements. (Note: these figures will be higher than those that appear in Tables 1 and 2, because they include net replacements which occur when workers retire or leave the profession.)

Registered Nurses (683,000)

Dental hygienists (104,000)

Pharmacists (64,000)

Physical therapists (94,000)

Physician assistants (39,000)

Occupational therapists (44,000)

Speech-language pathologists and audiologists (54,000)

Emergency medical technicians (96,000)

Medical assistants (210,000)

Health information technologists (61,000)

Licensed Practical Nurses (296,000)*

Physicians (197,000)*

Dentists (47,000)*

Registered Nurses (RNs)

According to the American Nurses Association, nurses are the largest group of health care providers in the country. Unlike physicians, who are primarily concerned with curing the patient, nursing is interested in the care of the patient and the family's response to illness. It is a holistic approach that focuses on prevention and wellness.

The Job

Nurses provide care for the sick and injured and help people stay well. They observe, assess, and record symptoms, reactions, and progress; assist physicians during treatments and examinations; administer medications; and assist in convalescence and rehabilitation.

State laws regulate the tasks registered nurses may perform. But what they do on a daily basis is usually related to their work setting.

Hospital nurses, the largest group of nurses, provide bedside nursing care and carry out the medical regimen prescribed by physicians. They may also supervise licensed practical nurses and aides. Hospital nurses usually are assigned to one area such as surgery, maternity, pediatrics, emergency room, intensive care, or treatment of cancer patients, or they may rotate among these departments.

Office nurses work for physicians in private practice, clinics, surgical centers, emergency medical centers, and health maintenance organizations (HMOs). Their job is to prepare patients for examinations, administer injections and medications, dress

---

*These jobs do not fit the criteria in Chapter 4 directly; they are covered indirectly in one or more of the following descriptions.

wounds and incisions, assist with minor surgery, and maintain records. They also assist the physician during examinations.

Home health nurses provide care according to a physician's instructions to homebound patients who may be recovering from illnesses and accidents, cancer, or childbirth.

Nursing home nurses manage nursing care for residents with conditions ranging from a fracture to Alzheimer's disease. While they generally spend most of their time on administrative and supervisory tasks, RNs also assess residents' medical condition, develop treatment plans, supervise licensed practical nurses and nursing aides, and perform difficult procedures such as starting intravenous fluids.

Public health nurses work in government and private agencies and clinics, schools, and retirement communities. They teach individuals and their families how to prevent diseases, get proper nutrition, and provide adequate child care. They also arrange for health screenings.

Occupational health or **industrial nurses** provide nursing care at work sites to employees, customers, and others with minor injuries and illnesses. **Head nurses** or **nurse supervisors** direct nursing activities. At the advanced level, **nurse practitioners** provide basic health care. They diagnose and treat common acute illnesses and injuries. Nurse practitioners can prescribe medications in some states. Other advanced practice nurses include **clinical nurse specialists**, **nurse anesthetists**, and **certified nurse-midwives**.

According to the Bureau of Labor Statistics, registered nurses held about 1,971,000 jobs in 1996. About two out of three work in hospitals. Others are employed in offices and clinics of physicians, home health care agencies, nursing homes, temporary help agencies, schools, and government agencies. More than one-fourth of all registered nurses work part-time.

Education/Training

Nurses must graduate from an accredited nursing school and pass a national licensing examination to obtain a nursing license in all states. Licenses must be periodically renewed. Some states require continuing education for licensure renewal.

There are three major educational paths:

Associate degree (ADN) at a community or junior college, which takes about 2 years.

Diploma given in hospitals usually in 2 to 3 years.

Bachelor of science degree (BSN) at colleges and universities (4 or 5 years).

Nurses who graduate from a BSN program generally have broader advancement opportunities. In fact, some career paths are open only to nurses who have bachelor's or advanced degrees.

While ADN or diploma preparation may be sufficient for a nursing-home nurse, a bachelor's degree is generally necessary for administrative positions in hospitals and for positions in community nursing. A BSN is a prerequisite for admission to graduate nursing programs in research, consulting, teaching, or a clinical specialization.

Career Mobility

In management, registered nurses can advance to assistant head nurse or head nurse. From there, they can advance to assistant director, director, and vice president.

In patient care, nurses can advance to clinical nurse specialist, nurse practitioner, certified nurse-midwife, or nurse anesthetist. These positions require one or two years of further graduate education, leading to a certificate or master's degree.

Desired Characteristics

Nurses should be caring and sympathetic. They need emotional stability to cope with human suffering, emergencies, and other stresses. They must be able to accept responsibility, direct or supervise others, follow orders precisely, and determine when consultation is required.

Job Outlook

Labor Department projections indicate that there will be 683,000 job openings for registered nurses between 1996 and 2006, due to growth and net replacements. Growth in employment will be driven by technological advances in patient care, and an increasing emphasis on primary care. Most rapid growth is expected in hospitals' outpatient facilities, such as same-day surgery, rehabilitation, and chemotherapy clinics. Employment in home health care is expected to grow the fastest.

In evolving integrated health care networks, nurses may rotate among employment settings. Since jobs in traditional hospital nursing positions are no longer the only option, RNs will need to be flexible. Opportunities will be best for nurses with advanced training.

Earnings

According to the Bureau of Labor Statistics, median weekly earnings of full-time salaried registered nurses were $697 in 1996. The middle 50 percent earned between $571 and $868. The lowest 10 percent earned less than $415; the top 10 percent, more than $1,039.

According to a Hay Group survey of HMOs, group practices, and hospital-based clinics, the median annual base salary of full-time nurse practitioners was $66,800 in 1996. The middle 50 percent earned between $54,200 and $69,200. Nurse-midwives earned about $70,100, and the middle 50 percent earned between $59,300 and $75,700. A Hay Group's survey of acute care hospitals revealed that the median annual base salary of full-time nurse anesthetists was $82,000 in 1997. The middle 50 percent earned between $74,700 and $90,300.

Staff RNs in chain nursing homes had median hourly earnings of $15.85 in 1996, according to the Buck Survey conducted by the American Health Care Association. The middle 50 percent earned between $14.03 and $17.73.

Many employers offer flexible work schedules, child care, educational benefits, and bonuses.

The Passion Factor: What do you like most about your occupation?

"I like seeing healthy, nine-year-old children who have been coming to the clinic since they were babies," says Alma Moreno*, a nurse at a public health clinic.

Having been a "sickly child," Moreno developed an interest in health care. As a college student, she had the opportunity to work in the intensive care unit of a hospital. "I was inspired by the compassion the nurses had for their patients. I admired their knowledge and found their work very motivating."

Related Occupations

Other workers who need similar skills are occupational therapists, paramedics, physical therapists, physician assistants, and respiratory therapists.

Additional Information

American Nurses Association
600 Maryland Avenue SW
Washington, DC 20024-2571

National League for Nursing
Communications Department
350 Hudson Street
New York, NY 10014

American Association of Colleges of Nursing
1 Dupont Circle, Suite 530
Washington, DC 20036

Hispanic Nurses Association
10111 Northwest Park Drive
Houston, TX 77086
(281) 591-8307
http://www.hispanicnurses.org

---

*Names that appear in all the "Passion" sections have been changed.

Dental Hygienists

As is the case with other occupations that involve health care delivery services, dental hygienists are needed to treat the rising number of Latinos who do not speak English. While it takes only about two-and-a-half years to obtain an associate's degree in this field, most programs are highly condensed and are considered difficult.

The Job

Dental hygienists clean teeth and help patients develop and maintain good oral health. For example, they may explain the relationship between diet and oral health, instruct patients as to how to select toothbrushes, and show them how to brush and floss their teeth. Hygienists examine patients' teeth and gums, noting any diseases or abnormalities. Using hand and rotary instruments, they remove calculus, stains, and plaque from teeth. They also take and develop dental X rays; and apply cavity preventive agents such as fluorides. In some states, hygienists administer local anesthesia and anesthetic gas; place and carve filling materials, temporary fillings, and periodontal dressings; remove sutures; and smooth and polish metal restorations.

Because dentists usually hire hygienists to work only two or three days a week, the job is particularly flexible. Full-time, part-time, evening, and weekend work is widely available. Hygienists may also hold jobs in more than one dental office.

Dental hygienists held about 133,000 jobs in 1996. More than half of all dental hygienists worked part-time, or less than thirty-five hours a week. While some hygienists work in public health agencies, hospitals, and clinics, the vast majority is employed in private dental offices.

Education/Training

Dental hygienists must be licensed by the state in which they practice. To qualify for licensure, candidates must graduate from an accredited dental hygiene school and pass both a written and clinical examination. The American Dental Association Joint Commission on National Dental Examinations administers the written examination that is accepted by all states and the District of Columbia. State or regional testing agencies administer the clinical examination. In addition, examinations on legal aspects of dental hygiene practice are required by most states. Alabama allows candidates to take its examination if they have been trained through a state-regulated on-the-job program in a dentist's office.

An associate degree is sufficient for practice in a private dental office. About half of the 230 accredited dental hygiene programs prefer applicants who have completed at least one year of college. Some of the bachelor's degree programs require applicants to have completed two years. However, requirements vary from school to school. These schools offer laboratory, clinical, and classroom instruction in subjects such as nutrition, radiography, histology (the study of tissue structure), periodontology (the study of gum diseases), pathology, dental materials, clinical dental hygiene, and social and behavioral sciences.

Career Mobility

Some dental hygienists go into private practice. Others choose to do research, teach, or go into clinical practice in public or school health programs. To do so they need a bachelor's or master's degree.

Desired Characteristics

Dental hygienists should be able to work well with others and must have good manual dexterity because they use dental instruments with little room for error within a patient's mouth. Their background should include knowledge of biology, chemistry, and mathematics.

Job Outlook

The Bureau of Labor Statistics projects that there will be 104,000 job openings for dental hygienists through the year 2006. Employment of dental hygienists is expected to grow in response to the increasing demand for dental care and the greater substitution of hygienists for services previously performed by dentists.

Demand also will be stimulated by population growth, and greater retention of natural teeth by the larger number of middle-aged and elderly people. In addition, as dentists' workloads increase, they are expected to hire more hygienists to perform preventive dental care such as cleaning. Also, as older dentists, who are less likely to employ dental hygienists than the more recent graduates, leave their practices, new positions for dental hygienists will be created.

Earnings

Earnings of dental hygienists are affected by geographic location, employment setting, education, and experience. Dental hygienists who work in private dental offices may be paid on an hourly, daily, salary, or commission basis. According to the American Dental Association, experienced dental hygienists who worked thirty-two hours a week or more in a private practice averaged about $759 a week in 1995.

Benefits vary substantially by practice setting, and may be contingent upon full-time employment. Dental hygienists who work for school systems, public health agencies, the federal government, or state agencies usually have substantial benefits.

The Passion Factor: What do you like most about your occupation?

"You leave a piece of you with each patient," says Renata Lanus, a hygienist who works in a private practice. "Motivating and educating the patients [about oral hygiene] is a daily challenge. You have to be a bit of a magician and somewhat of a comedian."

Born in Mexico, Lanus got interested in dentistry when her uncle married a dental surgeon. "In Mexico most dentists are women," she explained. "Here [in the U.S.] it is just the opposite."

The dentist for whom she works has benefited tremendously since he hired Lanus. "He had never had a hygienist in his practice before, and the number of Hispanic patients has tripled."

Related Occupations

Other occupations that require similar characteristics include dental assistants, ophthalmic medical assistants, podiatric medical assistants, office nurses, medical assistants, physician assistants, physical therapy assistants, and occupational therapy assistants.

Additional Information

Division of Professional Development
American Dental Hygienists' Association
444 N. Michigan Avenue, Suite 3400
Chicago, IL 60611
http://www.adha.org

Commission on Dental Accreditation
American Dental Association
211 E. Chicago Avenue, Suite 1814
Chicago, IL 60611
http://www.ada.org

The State Board of Dental Examiners in each state can supply information on licensing requirements.

Pharmacists

Pharmacists are moving beyond the traditional delivery of prescriptions and are becoming more involved in drug therapy decision-making and patient counseling. For that reason, it is even more important to have bilingual pharmacists serving the Latino community.

Debra Agard, a pharmacist and associate dean for student affairs in the College of Pharmacy at the University of Illinois at Chicago, characterizes the need for bilingual pharmacists as desperate. "How can you help patients understand how to take their medicine or explain the potential side effects when you can't speak the same language?" she asks. "The patients walk away in a daze and the pharmacist is left feeling very frustrated."

The Job

Pharmacists dispense drugs prescribed by physicians and other health practitioners and provide information to patients about medications and their use. But the actual mixing of ingredients to form powders, tablets, capsules, ointments, and solutions is only a small part of their practice. Most medicines are produced by pharmaceutical companies in a standard dosage and form. Pharmacists must understand the use, composition, and effects of drugs because they advise physicians and other health practitioners on the selection, dosages, interactions, and side effects of medications.

In community (retail) pharmacies, these professionals counsel patients, and answer questions about prescription drugs, such as possible adverse reactions and interactions. They provide information about over-the-counter drugs and make recommendations. Pharmacists also give advice about medical equipment and home health care supplies. Those who own or manage community pharmacies may buy and sell non-health-related merchandise, hire and supervise personnel, and oversee the general operation of the pharmacy. Some community pharmacists offer specialized disease state management services for conditions such as diabetes, asthma, smoking cessation, or high blood pressure.

In hospitals and clinics, pharmacists play several roles. They dispense medications and advise the medical staff on the selection and effects of drugs. They assess, plan, and monitor drug regimens. They also counsel patients on the use of drugs while in the hospital, and on their use at home when they are discharged. Pharmacists may also evaluate drug use patterns and outcomes in the hospital or in a patient population.

Pharmacists who work in home health care prepare medications for use in the home, and monitor drug therapy. Those who work in the increasingly popular mail-order pharmacies, process prescriptions for people who must take them regularly.

Most pharmacists keep computerized records of patients' drug therapies to ensure that harmful drug interactions do not occur. They frequently teach pharmacy students serving as externs in preparation for graduation and licensure.

Pharmacists held about 172,000 jobs in 1996. About three out of five worked in community pharmacies, either independently owned, part of a drugstore chain, or part of a grocery store, department store, or mass merchandiser. Approximately one out of five worked part-time.

Most community pharmacists were salaried employees, but some were self-employed owners. About one-quarter worked in hospitals, and others worked in clinics, mail-order pharmacies, pharmaceutical wholesalers, home health care agencies, or for the federal government.

Education/Training

All states require a license to practice pharmacy. To obtain a license, one must graduate from an accredited college of pharmacy, pass a state examination, and serve an internship under a licensed pharmacist. Many pharmacists are licensed to practice in more than one state. Most states require continuing education for license renewal.

Most pharmacists graduate with a bachelor of science in pharmacy, which takes five years beyond high school to complete. A doctor of pharmacy (PharmD) normally requires at least six years. Those who already hold the bachelor's degree may enter PharmD programs, but the combined period of study is usually longer than six years. By 1997, the number of schools offering the PharmD as the only professional degree had increased to forty-one, and the number offering the BS in pharmacy as the only professional degree continued to decline, with only four schools in 1998.

Most colleges of pharmacy require one or two years of college-level prepharmacy education. Some colleges require the applicant to take the Pharmacy College Admissions Test. Recently, pharmacy schools voted to move toward offering the PharmD as the only professional degree in pharmacy. All accredited pharmacy schools are expected to graduate their last BS class by the year 2004.

All colleges of pharmacy offer courses in pharmacy practice, designed to teach students to dispense prescriptions, communicate with patients and other health professionals, and to strengthen their understanding of professional ethics and practice management responsibilities. Pharmacists' training increasingly emphasizes direct patient care, as well as consultative services to other health professionals.

The bachelor's degree in pharmacy is generally acceptable for most positions in community pharmacies, at least in the foreseeable future. A growing number of hospital employers prefer that a pharmacist have a PharmD degree. A master's or PhD degree in pharmacy or a related field usually is required to do research, and a PharmD with additional residency or fellowship training, master's, or PhD usually is necessary for faculty positions.

Career Mobility

In community pharmacies, pharmacists usually begin at the staff level. With experience and capital, many become owners or part owners of pharmacies. Pharmacists in chain drugstores may be promoted to pharmacy supervisor or manager, at the store level, then at the district or regional level, and later to an executive position within the chain's headquarters.

Hospital pharmacists may advance to supervisory or administrative positions. Pharmacists in the pharmaceutical industry may advance in marketing, sales, research, quality control, production, packaging, and other areas.

Desired Characteristics

Pharmacists should have scientific aptitude, good communication skills, and a desire to help others. They must also be conscientious and pay close attention to detail, because the decisions they make affect human lives.

Job Outlook

The Bureau of Labor Statistics projects that there will be jobs for 64,000 pharmacists through the year 2006, due to growth and net replacements. The increased number of middle-aged and elderly people will spur demand for pharmacists in all practice settings. The number of prescriptions influences the demand for pharmacists, and the middle-aged and elderly population uses more prescription drugs, on average, than younger people.

Other factors likely to increase the demand for pharmacists include the likelihood of scientific advances that will make more drug products available, new developments in administering medication, and increasingly sophisticated consumers seeking more information about drugs.

As hospitals reduce inpatient stays, and downsize and consolidate departments, opportunities for pharmacists will be best in long-term, ambulatory, and home care settings. New opportunities for pharmacists are emerging in managed care organizations, where pharmacists analyze trends and patterns in medication use for their populations of patients.

Fast growth is also expected for pharmacists employed in research, disease management, and pharmacoeconomics determining the costs and benefits of different drug therapies.

With its emphasis on cost control, managed care has encouraged the growth of lower-cost distributors of prescription drugs such as mail-order firms. Slower employment growth is expected in traditional chain and independent pharmacies.

Earnings

The Bureau of Labor Statistics reports that the median weekly earnings of full-time, salaried pharmacists were $992 in 1996. Half earned between $827 and $1,177. The lowest 10 percent earned less than $554 and the top 10 percent more than $1,422.

According to a survey by *Drug Topics* magazine, published by Medical Economics, Inc., average base salaries of full-time, salaried pharmacists were $59,276 per year in 1996. Pharmacists working in chain drugstores had an average base salary of $61,735 per year, while pharmacists working in independent drugstores averaged $52,189, and hospital pharmacists averaged $61,317. Overall, salaries for pharmacists were highest in the West and second highest in the East. Many pharmacists also receive compensation in the form of bonuses, overtime, and profit-sharing.

The Passion Factor: What do you like most about your occupation?

"I like it when the customer appreciates what you are doing and realizes that, sometimes, waiting is worth their while," says Bob Marín, a registered pharmacist who recently switched jobs from a community to a mail-order pharmacy. "Many people don't realize that there are lots of details involved. A pharmacist has to do many things at the same time, like answer phones, and take care of the customers—without making a life-threatening mistake."

Marín was interested in doing something related to public service since he was very young. He also enjoyed math and science in school. "So pharmacy was a good choice of profession," he explains.

Related Occupations

Other professions that may require similar skills include pharmaceutical chemists, pharmacologists, medical scientists, and biological technicians.

Additional Information

American Association of Colleges of Pharmacy
1426 Prince Street
Alexandria, VA 22314

Information on specific college entrance requirements, curricula, and financial aid is available from the dean of any college of pharmacy.

Physical Therapists

"We have an urgent need for bilingual physical therapists," says Jules Rothstein, chief of physical therapy services at the University of Illinois Hospital, pointing out that it is very difficult to discuss a course of treatment with patients who do not speak English—even with the aid of a translator. "Spanish is the number one second language we need."

The Job

Physical therapists help improve mobility, relieve pain, and prevent or limit permanent physical disabilities of patients who suffer from injuries, such as accident victims, or disease, such as multiple sclerosis, cerebral palsy, or nerve injuries. They evaluate patients' medical histories, test and measure their strength, range of motion, and ability to function, and develop treatment plans.

Treatment, which often includes exercise for patients who have been immobilized and lack flexibility, is often carried out by physical therapy aides. Therapists increase the patient's flexibility by stretching and manipulating stiff joints and unused muscles. Later in the treatment, they encourage patients to use their own muscles to further increase flexibility and range of motion before finally advancing to weights and other exercises that improve strength, balance, coordination, and endurance.

Therapists also teach patients to use crutches, prostheses, and wheelchairs to perform day-to-day activities, and show them exercises to do at home to expedite their recovery. Some physical therapists treat a wide range of ailments; others specialize in areas such as pediatrics, geriatrics, orthopedics, sports medicine, neurology, and cardiopulmonary physical therapy.

According to the Bureau of Labor Statistics, physical therapists held about 115,000 jobs in 1996. About one in four work part-time. Hospitals employ one-third, and offices of physical therapists employ about one-quarter of all salaried physical therapists. Other jobs are in offices of physicians, home health care agencies, nursing homes, and schools. Some physical therapists are self-employed in private practices.

Education/Training

All states require physical therapists to pass a licensure exam after graduating from an accredited physical therapy program, before they can practice.

A bachelor's degree in physical therapy is required. Individuals who have a four-year degree in a related field, such as genetics or biology, and want to become physical therapists should enroll in a master's level physical therapy program. Before granting admission, many educational programs require volunteer experience in the physical therapy department of a hospital or clinic.

Career Mobility

Physical therapists can be promoted to an administrative position, or attain a research or teaching job. A master's degree is recommended for those positions.

Desired Characteristics

Physical therapists must have strong interpersonal skills to treat patients and deal with their families. They should be compassionate, and have manual dexterity and physical stamina.

Job Outlook

According to the Bureau of Labor Statistics, there will be 94,000 jobs for physical therapists through the year 2006, due to growth and net replacements. The rapidly growing elderly population, which is particularly vulnerable to chronic and debilitating conditions requiring therapeutic services, will be one of the factors resulting in employment growth.

Baby boomers, who are entering the prime age for heart attacks and strokes, will increase the demand for cardiac and physical rehabilitation. As well, medical advances that save the lives of a larger proportion of newborns with severe birth defects will necessitate the services of physical therapists.

The widespread interest in health promotion should also increase demand for physical therapy services. A growing number of employers are using physical therapists to evaluate work sites, develop exercise programs, and teach safe work habits to employees in the hope of reducing injuries.

Earnings

The Bureau of Labor Statistics reports that the median weekly earnings of salaried physical therapists who usually work full-time were $757 in 1996. The middle 50 percent earned between $577 and $1,055. The top 10 percent earned at least $1,294 and the bottom 10 percent earned less than $400.

According to the American Physical Therapy Association's survey of physical therapists practicing in hospital settings, the median annual base salary of full-time physical therapists was $48,000 in 1996. The middle 50 percent earned $42,000 and $57,000.

Physical therapists in private practice tend to earn more than salaried workers. Also, many sources report that salaries are higher in rural areas as employers try to attract therapists to areas experiencing severe shortages.

The Passion Factor: What do you like most about your occupation?

"It is very rewarding to see the progression of a patient, from a wheelchair to a cane, to walking freely," says Mimi Martínez, a physical therapist employed in a private hospital.

Since she was a child in Guatemala, Martínez always thought she would attend medical school. When she began to volunteer in different health care settings, she realized she liked to have extensive contact with patients. "As a physical therapist, you develop a long-term relationship with your patients," she explains. "It is much more intense because you may see them three times a week for one hour over the course of three months."

Related Occupations

Other workers with similar skills include occupational therapists, corrective therapists, recreational therapists, manual arts therapists, speech pathologists and audiologists, prosthetists, respiratory therapists, chiropractors, acupuncturists, and athletic trainers.

Additional Information

> American Physical Therapy Association
> 1111 N. Fairfax Street
> Alexandria, VA 22314-1488

Physician Assistants

Among the fastest growing occupations, the number of physician assistants is projected to increase 47 percent between 1996 and 2006. Earnings are high and job opportunities are expected to be excellent.

The Job

Physician assistants (PAs) are formally trained to provide diagnostic, therapeutic, and preventive health care services under the supervision of a physician. They should not be confused with **medical assistants**, who perform routine clinical and clerical tasks (a description of that occupation appears later in this chapter). PAs take medical histories, examine patients, order and interpret laboratory tests and X rays, and make diagnoses. They also treat minor injuries by suturing, splinting, and casting. PAs record progress notes, instruct and counsel patients, and order or carry out therapy. In thirty-nine states and the District of Columbia, physician assistants may prescribe medications. PAs may also have managerial duties. Some order medical and laboratory supplies and equipment, while others supervise technicians and assistants.

Physician assistants always work under the supervision of a physician. However, the extent of supervision varies according to state laws. In rural or inner city clinics, for example, a PA may provide care when a physician is present only one or two days each week, but consulting with the supervising physician and other medical professionals as needed or required by law. PAs may also make house calls or go to hospitals and nursing homes to check on patients and report back to the physician.

Depending on the state where they practice, the duties of a physician assistant may be determined by the supervising physician, or by the state's regulatory agency. Some PAs work in primary care areas such as general internal medicine, pediatrics, and family practice. Others work in specialty areas, such as general surgery, emergency medicine, orthopedics, and geriatrics. PAs specializing in surgery provide pre- and postoperative care and may work as first or second assistants during major surgery.

According to the Bureau of Labor Statistics, physician assistants held about 64,000 jobs in 1996. Sixty-six percent worked in the offices and clinics of physicians, dentists, or other health practitioners. Approximately 20 percent were employed by hospitals. The rest were mostly in public health clinics, nursing homes, prisons, home health care agencies, and the Department of Veterans Affairs.

According to the American Academy of Physician Assistants, about one-third of all PAs provide health care to communities having fewer than 50,000 residents, where physicians may be in limited supply.

Education/Training

To become a PA, candidates must complete an accredited, formal education program in almost every state. In 1997, some educational programs for physician assistants offered a baccalaureate degree or a degree option. Others offered either a certificate, an associate's degree, or a master's degree. Most PA graduates have at least a bachelor's degree.

Admission requirements vary, but many programs require two years of college and some work experience in the health care field. More than half of all applicants hold a bachelor's or master's degree. Many are former emergency medical technicians, other allied health professionals, or nurses.

PA programs generally last two years. Most are in schools of allied health, academic health centers, medical schools, or four-year colleges; a few are in community colleges, the military, or hospitals. Many accredited PA programs have clinical teaching affiliations with medical schools.

Students obtain supervised clinical training in several areas, including primary care medicine, inpatient medicine, surgery, obstetrics and gynecology, geriatrics, emergency medicine, psychiatry, and pediatrics. Sometimes, PA students serve one or more of these "rotations" under the supervision of a physician who is seeking to hire a PA. These rotations often lead to permanent employment.

As of 1997, forty-nine states and the District of Columbia had legislation governing the qualifications or practice of physician assistants. Mississippi did not. Forty-nine states required physician assistants to pass the Physician Assistants National Certifying Examination that is only open to graduates of an accredited educational program. In order to remain certified, PAs must complete 100 hours of continuing medical education every two years. Every six years, they must pass a recertification examination or complete an alternate program combining learning experiences and a take-home examination.

Career Mobility

Some PAs pursue additional education in order to practice in a specialty area such as surgery, neonatology, or emergency medicine. Others, as they attain greater clinical knowledge and experience, advance to added responsibilities and higher earnings. However, by the very nature of the profession, individual PAs are usually supervised by physicians.

Desired Characteristics

Physician assistants must have leadership skills, self-confidence, and emotional stability. They must be willing to continue studying throughout their career to keep up with medical advances.

Job Outlook

The Bureau of Labor Statistics estimates that there will be 39,000 job openings for physician assistants through the year 2006, due to growth and net replacements. Demand will be spurred by the anticipated expansion of the health services industry and an emphasis on cost containment. Because PAs are cost-effective and productive members of the health care team, physicians and institutions are expected to employ additional PAs to provide primary care and assist with medical and surgical procedures.

Telemedicine—the use of technology to facilitate interactive consultations between physicians and physician assistants—will also expand the utilization of physician assistants. Besides the traditional office-based setting, PAs should find a growing number of jobs in institutional settings such as hospitals, academic medical centers, public clinics, and prisons.

State-imposed legal limitations on the number of hours worked by physician residents are increasingly common and encourage hospitals to use PAs to supply some physician resident services.

Opportunities will be best in states that allow PAs a wider scope of practice, such as the ability to prescribe medication, especially in areas that have difficulty attracting physicians, such as rural and inner-city clinics.

Earnings

According to the American Academy of Physician Assistants, the median income for physician assistants in full-time clinical practice in 1996 was $60,687; median income for first year graduates was $52,116. Income varies by specialty, practice setting, geographical location, and years of experience.

According to a Hay Group survey of HMOs, group practices, and hospital-based clinics, the median annual base salary of full-time physician assistants was $54,100 in 1996. The middle 50 percent earned between $49,100 and $60,000. The average annual salary for physician assistants employed by the federal government was $48,670 in early 1997.

The Passion Factor: What do you like most about your occupation?

"This is quite a satisfying profession because you get very involved with patient care," exclaims Marta Rodríguez, a PA who works at a public health clinic. "You not only treat the patient, but you also educate him about his ailment."

Rodríguez knew she would choose a career in the medical field, "ever since I can remember." But as a medical assistant at the same clinic where she now works, she realized she couldn't participate actively in the care of patients. "Then I found out that I could become a physician assistant and I went for it."

Related Occupations

Other occupations that require similar skills include nurse practitioners, physical therapists, occupational therapists, clinical psychologists, speech-language pathologists, and audiologists.

Additional Information

American Academy of Physician Assistants Information
    Center
950 N. Washington Street
Alexandria, VA 22314-1552
http://www.aapa.org

Association of Physician Assistant Programs
950 N. Washington Street
Alexandria, VA 22314-1552

National Commission on Certification of Physician
    Assistants, Inc.
6849-B2 Peachtree Dunwoody Road
Atlanta, GA 30328

Occupational Therapists

As is the case with physical therapy, there is a great need for bilingual occupational therapists who can help their Spanish-speaking patients recover and return to work.

The Job

Occupational therapists help people with mentally, physically, developmentally, or emotionally disabling conditions to develop, recover, or maintain daily living and work skills. Their goal is to help patients lead independent, productive, and satisfying lives.

Activities range from helping the patient use a computer to caring for daily needs, such as dressing, cooking, and eating. Physical exercises may be used to increase strength and dexterity, while paper and pencil games may be chosen to improve visual acuity and the ability to discern patterns. Computer programs have been designed to help patients improve their ability to make decisions, or use abstract reasoning, problem solving, and perceptual skills, as well as memory, sequencing, and coordination—all of which are necessary for independent living.

Therapists provide adaptive equipment such as wheelchairs, splints, and aids for eating and dressing, for patients with permanent functional disabilities, such as spinal cord injuries, cerebral palsy, or muscular dystrophy. They also may design or make special equipment for use at home or at work. Therapists develop and teach patients to operate computer-aided adaptive equipment, such as microprocessing devices that permit individuals with severe limitations to communicate, walk, operate telephones and television sets, and control other aspects of their environment.

According to the Bureau of Labor Statistics, occupational therapists held about 57,000 jobs in 1996. Most work in hospitals, particularly in rehabilitation and psychiatric hospitals. School systems are the second largest employer of occupational therapists. Other major employers include offices of occupational therapists and other health practitioners, nursing homes, community mental health centers, adult day care programs, job training services, and residential care facilities. A small but rapidly growing number of occupational therapists are in private practice.

Education/Training

A bachelor's degree in occupational therapy is the minimum requirement. Thirty-nine states, Puerto Rico, and the District of

Columbia require a license (applicants must have a degree or a post-bachelor's certificate from an accredited educational program, and pass a national certification examination given by the American Occupational Therapy Certification Board). Those who pass the test are awarded the title of registered occupational therapist.

Occupational therapy course work includes physical, biological, and behavioral sciences, and the application of occupational therapy theory and skills. Completion of six months of supervised fieldwork is also required.

Desired Characteristics

Occupational therapists need warmth and patience to inspire their patients' trust. Ingenuity and imagination in adapting activities to individual needs are assets. The ability to successfully adapt to a variety of settings is also a plus.

Job Outlook

According to the Bureau of Labor Statistics, there will be 44,000 jobs for occupational therapists through the year 2006, due to growth and net replacements. Growth in demand will stem from medical advances which are now making it possible for more patients with critical problems to survive but often needing extensive therapy. Also, the baby-boom generation is moving into middle age—a period during which the incidence of heart attack and stroke increases. In addition, the rapidly growing population seventy-five years of age and above, which suffers from a very high incidence of disabling conditions, will contribute to the demand for occupational therapists.

Due to industry growth and more intensive care, hospitals will continue to employ the largest number of occupational therapists. Hospitals will also need occupational therapists to staff their growing home health care and outpatient rehabilitation programs.

Earnings

As reported by the Bureau of Labor Statistics, median weekly earnings of full-time salaried occupational therapists were $780 in

1996. The middle 50 percent earned between $622 and $982. The lowest 10 percent earned less than $479; the top 10 percent earned more than $1,116.

According to a Hay Group survey of acute care hospitals, the median annual base salary of full-time occupational therapists was $42,700 in 1997. The middle 50 percent earned between $39,100 and $46,100.

The Passion Factor: What do you like most about your occupation?

"The reward is to see my patients returning to work," says Luis Gonzaléz, an occupational therapist working for a private practice.

Convinced since he was young that he was on this earth "for a good reason," Gonzaléz explored the possibility of becoming a priest before choosing to become an occupational therapist. Ten years later, he is convinced that "this is my calling."

Related Occupations

Workers who need similar skills are prosthetists, physical therapists, chiropractors, speech pathologists and audiologists, rehabilitation counselors, recreational therapists, art therapists, music therapists, dance therapists, horticultural therapists, and manual arts therapists.

Additional Information

The American Occupational Therapy Association
4720 Montgomery Lane
PO Box 31220
Bethesda, MD 20824-1220

Speech-Language Pathologists and Audiologists

"We need bilingual pathologists, especially for the older adults with strokes who only speak Spanish," says Tricia Chambers, a speech and language pathology professor at St. Xavier University. "But [to be a good bilingual pathologist] you also need to spend some time formally studying the structure of your own language."

The Job

Speech-language pathologists assess and treat persons with speech, language, voice, and fluency disorders. They work with people who cannot make speech sounds, or cannot make them clearly; those with speech rhythm and fluency problems, such as stuttering; people with speech quality problems, such as inappropriate pitch or harsh voice; and those with problems understanding and producing language. They may also work with people who have oral motor problems that cause eating and swallowing difficulties. Speech and language problems may result from causes such as hearing loss, brain injury or deterioration, cerebral palsy, stroke, cleft palate, voice pathology, mental retardation, or emotional problems.

Audiologists assess and treat those with hearing and related disorders. They use audiometers and other testing devices to measure the loudness at which a person begins to hear sounds, the ability to distinguish between sounds, and other tests of the nature and extent of their hearing loss. Audiologists may coordinate these results with medical, educational, and psychological information, make a diagnosis, and determine a course of treatment. Hearing disorders may result from causes such as viral infections, genetic disorders, or exposure to loud noise.

The majority of speech-language pathologists and audiologists provide direct clinical services to individuals with communication disorders.

According to the Bureau of Labor Statistics, speech-language pathologists and audiologists held about 87,000 jobs in 1996. About one-half of speech-language pathologists and audiologists provide services in preschools, elementary and secondary schools, or colleges and universities. More than 10 percent work in hospitals. Others work in physicians' offices, or speech, language, and hearing centers. Some are in private practice.

Training/Education

A master's degree in speech-language pathology or audiology is required, but by the year 2005 a doctoral degree may be required for entry into the audiology practice.

Of the forty-five states that regulate speech-language pathologists and/or audiologists, all currently require a master's degree or equivalent, 300 to 375 hours of supervised clinical experience, a passing score on a national examination, and nine months of post-graduate professional experience. In some states, people with bachelor's degrees in speech-language pathology may work in schools with students who have communication problems (but may be classified as special education teachers).

Those with a master's degree can acquire the Certificate of Clinical Competence (CCC) offered by the American Speech-Language-Hearing Association or the Fellowship-AAA (F-AAA) offered by the American Academy of Audiology.

Desired Characteristics

Speech-language pathologists and audiologists should be able to effectively communicate test results, diagnoses, and proposed treatment in a manner easily understood by their clients. They must have the ability to approach problems objectively and provide support to clients and their families. Patience and compassion also are important because a client's progress may be slow.

Career Mobility

With experience, some salaried speech-language pathologists and audiologists enter private practice; others become directors or administrators of services in schools, hospitals, health departments, and clinics. Some become researchers.

Job Outlook

Department of Labor projections indicate that there will be 54,000 openings for speech-language pathologists and audiologists through the year 2006, due to growth and net replacements. Employment demand will be spurred by the rapid growth in the population age seventy-five and over, and the increased number of hearing-impaired persons. Also, as baby boomers enter middle age, they face the possibility of neurological disorders and an increase in associated speech, language, and hearing impairments.

Employment in elementary and secondary schools will increase because federal law guarantees special education and related services to all eligible children with disabilities.

The number of speech-language pathologists and audiologists in private practice, though small, is likely to rise sharply by the year 2005. Encouraging this growth is the increasing use of contract services by hospitals, schools, and nursing homes.

Earnings

According to the Bureau of Labor Statistics, median weekly earnings of full-time salaried speech-language pathologists and audiologists were about $690 in 1996. The middle 50 percent earned between $560 and $880. The lowest 10 percent earned less than $440 and the top 10 percent more than $1,160.

Results of a 1997 survey by the American Speech-Language-Hearing Association showed that the median annual salary for full-time certified speech-language pathologists was $44,000; for audiologists, $43,000. Certified speech-language pathologists with one to three years of experience earned a median annual salary of $38,000; licensed audiologists with one to three years of experience earned $32,000. Speech-language pathologists with twenty-two years of experience earned a median annual salary of $52,000, while audiologists with comparable experience earned about $55,000. Salaries also vary according to geographic location and type of employment facility.

The Passion Factor: What do you like most about your occupation?

"That I work with kids and get closure every day," says Peter Smith, a speech-language pathologist working in a public school system.

Smith, who was born in the United States but lived in Colombia for many years, is completely bilingual and bicultural. He became interested in speech-language pathology in college, when he took a course on the subject and met the inspirational professor who taught it. Upon graduation, "I took this job temporarily," he recounts. That was twenty-two years ago.

Related Occupations

Workers who use similar skills include occupational therapists, optometrists, physical therapists, psychologists, recreational therapists, and rehabilitation counselors.

Additional Information

American Speech-Language-Hearing Association
10801 Rockville Pike
Rockville, MD 20852

American Academy of Audiology
1735 N. Lynn Street #900
Arlington, VA 22209

Emergency Medical Technicians

Emergency medical technicians (EMTs) depend on the victims to describe what just took place. If they encounter a life-threatening situation—as they often do—the language barrier could mean the difference between life and death.

The Job

Emergency medical technicians give immediate care and often transport the sick or injured to medical facilities. Typically, EMTs are called to provide urgent medical attention to the victims of automobile accidents, heart attacks, near drownings, unscheduled childbirths, poisonings, and gunshot wounds.

EMTs usually work in teams of two and drive specially equipped vehicles to the scene of emergencies. They determine the nature and extent of the patient's injuries or illness while also trying to determine whether the patient has other preexisting medical conditions. EMTs must follow strict guidelines and only perform those procedures for which they are certified. However, all EMTs (including **EMT-basics**) may open airways, restore breathing, control bleeding, treat for shock, administer oxygen, immobilize fractures, bandage wounds, assist in childbirth, manage emotionally disturbed patients, treat and assist heart attack victims, give initial care to poison and burn victims, and use automated external defibrillators to assist in the care of patients experiencing cardiac arrest.

The training provided to **EMT-intermediates** is more advanced, allowing them to administer intravenous fluids; use manual defibrillators to give lifesaving shocks to a stopped heart; use advanced airway techniques and equipment to assist patients experiencing respiratory emergencies, as well as use other intensive care procedures.

EMT-paramedics provide the most extensive pre-hospital care. In addition to the procedures already described, paramedics may administer drugs orally and intravenously, interpret electrocardiograms (EKGs), perform endotracheal intubations, and use monitors and other complex equipment.

EMTs usually handle simple conditions by following general rules and guidelines. More complicated problems can only be carried out under the step-by-step direction of medical personnel by radio contact.

When transporting patients to a medical facility, EMTs may use special equipment such as backboards to immobilize patients before placing them on stretchers and securing them in the ambulance. While one EMT drives, the other monitors the patient's vital signs and gives additional care as needed. Some EMTs work for hospital trauma centers or jurisdictions which use helicopters to transport critically ill or injured patients. At a medical facility, EMTs transfer patients to the emergency department, report to the staff their observations and the care they provided, and help administer emergency treatment.

According to the Bureau of Labor Statistics, EMTs held about 150,000 jobs in 1996. About two-fifths were in private ambulance services; a third were in municipal fire, police, or rescue squad departments; and a quarter were in hospitals. In addition, there are many volunteer EMTs. Most paid EMTs work in metropolitan areas. In many smaller cities, towns, and rural areas, there are more volunteer positions than paid EMT jobs.

Education/Training

Formal EMT training, which is needed to practice in this occupation, is available in all fifty states and the District of Columbia, and is offered by police, fire, and health departments; in hospitals; and as non-degree courses in colleges and universities. Training consists of three progressive levels, EMT-basic, EMT-intermediate, and EMT-paramedic. Fully qualified technicians complete all three programs. In some cases, First Responder training programs may qualify individuals for entry-level jobs. These programs provide emergency medical basics for firefighters, police officers, and others whose jobs make them likely to be the first persons to arrive at an incident scene. However, continued employment requires completion of EMT training. In addition to EMT training, EMTs in fire and police departments must be qualified as firefighters or police officers.

The EMT-basic is the minimum training needed. It entails 110 to 120 hours of classroom work plus ten hours of internship in a hospital emergency room. The program provides instruction and practice in dealing with common problems EMTs encounter in their victims, such as bleeding, fractures, airway obstruction, cardiac arrest, and emergency childbirth. Students also learn to use and care for common emergency equipment, such as suction devices, splints, oxygen delivery systems, and stretchers. Graduates of approved EMT-basic training programs earn the title of registered EMT-basic when they pass a written and practical examination administered by the state certifying agency or the National Registry of Emergency Medical Technicians.

Although requirements for EMT-intermediate training vary from state to state, training typically includes thirty-five to fifty-five hours of additional instruction beyond EMT-basic and covers patient evaluation as well as the use of advanced airway devices, and intravenous fluids. Prerequisites for taking the EMT-intermediate examination include classroom work, and a specified amount of clinical experience and field internship.

The majority of EMT-intermediates continue their education and receive the EMT-paramedic certification. EMT-paramedic training programs generally last between 750 and 2,000 hours. Most EMT-paramedics are in paid positions. Refresher courses and continuing education are available for EMTs at all levels.

In most states, registration for EMT-paramedics by the National Registry of Emergency Medical Technicians or a state emergency medical services agency requires state certification. Although not a general requirement for employment, registration acknowledges an EMT-paramedic's qualifications and makes higher paying jobs easier to obtain. All fifty states possess a certification procedure.

Career Mobility

An EMT-paramedic can become a supervisor, operations manager, administrative director, or executive director of emergency services. Some EMTs become EMT instructors, firefighters, dispatchers, or physician assistants, while others move into sales or marketing of emergency medical equipment. Finally, some become EMTs to assess their interest in health care and then decide to return to school and become registered nurses, physicians, or other health workers.

Desired Characteristics

EMTs should be emotionally stable to deal with the stress which arises in a job that involves life-or-death situations. They also should have good dexterity, agility, and physical coordination, and be able to lift and carry heavy loads. EMTs need good eyesight with accurate color vision.

Job Outlook

The Bureau of Labor Statistics projects that there will be 96,000 job openings for EMTs through the year 2006, due to growth and net replacements. Demand will be driven by an expanding population, particularly in older age groups that are the greatest users of emergency medical services. Additional job openings will occur as more states begin to allow EMT-paramedics to perform primary care on the scene without transporting the patient to a medical facility. As well, growth will occur as positions change from volunteer to paid positions.

Competition for jobs will be keen in fire, police, and rescue squad departments because of attractive pay and benefits and good job security. Opportunities for EMTs are expected to be excellent in hospitals and private ambulance services, where pay and benefits usually are low.

Average Annual Salaries of Emergency Medical Technicians, by Type of Employer, 1996

Employer	EMT-basic	EMT-paramedic
All employers	$25,051	$30,407
Fire departments	29,859	32,483
Hospital based	18,686	28,373
Private ambulance services	18,617	23,995

Source: *Journal of Emergency Medical Services*

Earnings

Earnings of EMTs depend on the employment setting and geographic location as well as the individual's training and experience. According to the 1996 *Journal of Emergency Medical Services* salary survey, average salaries were $25,051 for EMT-basic, and $30,407 for EMT-paramedic. EMTs working in fire departments command the highest salaries, as the accompanying table shows.

Those in emergency medical services who are part of fire or police departments receive the same benefits as firefighters or police officers.

The Passion Factor: What do you like most about your occupation?

"This is the most meaningful job I have ever had," states Joe Salinas, who has been an EMT-paramedic for the last twenty years. "I start the healing process for people who are sick or injured," he continues. "I am the first person they see who can relieve their pain and help them or their families understand what's going on. Sometimes, it is just a matter of holding a hand."

Salinas, who is also a paramedic instructor in his city's fire department, gave up a better-paying human services job when he met a paramedic who changed the course of his life. "We talked for ten minutes and I was so impressed with what he did that I decided I would do it as well," he recalls. "It is a challenging job, but very worthwhile. We [paramedics] can organize a life that is in total disarray and help make some sense out of it."

Related Occupations

Other occupations that require similar skills include police officers, firefighters, air traffic controllers, workers in other health occupations, and members of the armed forces.

Additional Information

National Association of Emergency Medical Technicians
408 Monroe
Clinton, MS 39056

National Registry of Emergency Medical Technicians
PO Box 29233
Columbus, OH 43229

Information concerning training courses, registration, and job opportunities for EMTs can be obtained by writing to the State Emergency Medical Service Director.

Medical Assistants

Medical assistants are usually the first health care professionals a patient encounters in a clinic or doctor's office. Their ability to make patients feel at ease is important, as is the language they speak. Trust is gained much faster when patients can communicate their problems and concerns in their native language.

The Job

Medical assistants perform routine clinical and clerical tasks to keep the offices of physicians, podiatrists, chiropractors, and optometrists running smoothly.

Their duties vary from office to office—depending on office location, size, and specialty—and range from answering telephones to drawing blood, and arranging for hospital admission and laboratory services. Those who have specialties carry additional duties and include **podiatric** and **ophthalmic medical assistants**.

According to the Bureau of Labor Statistics, medical assistants held about 225,000 jobs in 1996. Seven in ten jobs are in physicians' offices, and over one in ten are in offices of other health practitioners such as chiropractors, optometrists, and podiatrists. The rest are in hospitals, nursing homes, and other health care facilities.

Education/Training

This is probably the only occupation in the medical field which is open to individuals with no formal training. Usually, they need a high school diploma or the equivalent, with courses in mathematics, health, biology, computers, and office skills. Volunteer experience in the health care field is also helpful.

Formal programs in medical assisting are offered in vocational or technical high schools, post-secondary vocational schools, community and junior colleges, and in colleges and universities.

Certified applicants take a national examination. The American Association of Medical Assistants awards the Certified Medical Assistant credential; the American Medical Technologists awards the Registered Medical Assistant credential.

Desired Characteristics

Medical assistants must have a courteous, pleasant manner, and be able to put patients at ease. They must respect the confidential nature of medical information. Clinical duties require a reasonable level of manual dexterity and visual acuity.

Career Mobility

Medical assistants may be able to advance to office manager or may qualify for a wide variety of administrative support occupations. Some, with additional education, enter other health occupations such as nursing and medical technology.

Job Outlook

The Bureau of Labor Statistics projects that 210,000 jobs will be available for medical assistants through the year 2006, due to growth and net replacements. Employment growth will be driven by growth in the number of group practices, clinics, and other health care facilities that need a high proportion of support personnel.

The best job prospects are for those with formal training or experience, particularly those with certification.

Earnings

The earnings of medical assistants vary widely, depending on experience, skill level, and location. According to the *1997 Staff Salary Survey* published by the Health Care Group, average hourly wages for medical assistants with less than two years of experience ranged from $8.07 to $10.90 in 1996. Average hourly wages for medical assistants with more than five years of experience ranged from $10.38 to $13.46. Wages were higher in the Northeast and West and lower in the Midwest and South.

The Passion Factor: What do you like most about your occupation?

"I like my job because the patients feel like family to me," says Ana María López, who works for a private group of internists. "I have worked here for so long that I have seen many of the children grow up."

Loyalty, like López feels toward her employer, is somewhat unusual these days. "But why would you change jobs when you look forward to going to work every morning?"

Related Occupations

Workers who use similar skills are hospital admitting clerks, pharmacy helpers, medical record clerks, dental assistants, occupational therapy aides, and physical therapy aides.

Additional Information

The American Association of Medical Assistants
20 N. Wacker Drive, Suite 1575
Chicago, IL 60606-2903

Health Information Technologists

"In an urban setting, being bilingual can be an asset for health information technologists," says Cindy DeBerg, chair of the Health Information Technology Department at Oakton Community College in Illinois. (The name of this occupation was changed from **Medical Records Technicians** to reflect its more recently computerized nature.)

The Job

Health information technologists organize, evaluate, and code all medical records for completeness and accuracy. These records are notes made each time health care personnel treat a patient, and include information the patients provide about their symptoms and medical history, as well as the results of examinations, X-ray reports and laboratory tests, and diagnoses and treatment plans.

Duties vary with the size of the facility. In large to medium facilities, these technologists may specialize in one aspect of medical records or supervise medical records clerks and transcribers while a **medical records administrator** manages the department. In small facilities, a health Accredited Record Technologist may manage the department.

According to the Bureau of Labor Statistics, health information technologists held about 87,000 jobs in 1996. About half of them work in hospitals. Most of the remainder are employed in nursing homes, medical group practices, health maintenance organizations, and clinics. In addition, insurance, accounting, and law firms that deal in health matters employ medical record technologists to tabulate and analyze data from medical records. Public health departments hire technologists to supervise data collection from health care institutions and to assist in research.

Education/Training

Two-year associate degree programs are offered at community and junior colleges. Applicants can improve their chances of admission into a program by taking biology, chemistry, health, and computer courses in high school.

Technologists may also gain training through an Independent Study Program in Medical Record Technology offered by the American Health Information Management Association (AHIMA). Most employers prefer to hire Accredited Record Technologists (ART). Accreditation is obtained by passing a written examination offered by the AHIMA. To take the examination, a person must be a graduate of a two-year associate degree program accredited by the Commission on Accreditation of Allied Health Education Programs (CAAHEP) of the American Medical Association, or a graduate of the Independent Study Program in Medical Record Technology who has also obtained thirty semester hours of academic credit in prescribed areas.

Career Mobility

Experienced technologists generally advance by either specializing or managing. Many senior medical record technologists specialize in coding, particularly Medicare coding, or in tumor registry.

In large medical record departments, experienced technologists may become section supervisors, overseeing the work of the coding, correspondence, or discharge sections, for example. Senior technologists with ART credentials may become director or assistant director of a medical record department in a small facility. However, in larger institutions the director is a health information administrator, with a bachelor's degree in medical record administration.

Desired Characteristics

In this highly computerized discipline, technologists must be detail-oriented, and feel very comfortable with the use and application of technology.

Job Outlook

Department of Labor projections indicate that there will be jobs for 61,000 health information technologists through the year 2006, due to growth and net replacements. Employment will increase due to rapid growth in the number of medical tests, treatments, and procedures. Because medical records will be increasingly scrutinized by third-party payers, courts, and consumers this may also boost demand.

Faster employment growth is expected to occur in large group practices, offices of specialists, and in health maintenance organizations.

Earnings

According to a 1996 survey by the American Health Information Management Association, the median annual salary for accredited health information technologists was $31,200 a year. The average annual salary for health information technologists employed by the federal government was $25,570 in early 1997.

The Passion Factor: What do you like most about your occupation?

"Every case is different, so you learn a lot in the process," says Marta Serrano, a registered record administrator at a private hospital. "And every day is a different day, so I am never bored."

Serrano always had been interested in the health care field and actually began taking classes in order to become a registered nurse. "But then I realized that I didn't want to have direct patient contact so I changed my major."

Related Occupations

Workers who use similar skills are medical secretaries, medical transcribers, medical writers, and medical illustrators.

Additional Information

American Health Information Management Association
919 N. Michigan Avenue, Suite 1400
Chicago, IL 60611

Financial Services Careers

The median U.S. Latino household income has more than doubled since 1980. Strategy Research Corporation estimates that it is now at $40,200 per year, and that our combined buying power is over $273 billion. With more disposable income, Latinos are buying houses, cars, and insurance policies. Many have enough left over to invest. Those of us who are bilingual and feel attracted to the world of finance ought to consider exploring the financial services field, which includes banking, securities, and accounting.

"The opportunities in this field are phenomenal," says Francisco Gutierrez, a financial planner who works for a large investment firm. "My company has 300 financial planners in the area and only four of us are Hispanic—and only three of us speak Spanish."

Even if you don't speak Spanish, the field of financial services is very promising. The Bureau of Labor Statistics estimates that there will be 124,000 jobs for securities and financial sales workers between now and 2006. As the baby boomers begin to plan for their old age, they will seek the advice of professionals who can help them invest their money wisely so their children can attend college and they can have a comfortable retirement.

In this chapter, we will focus on the following occupations (figures in parenthesis represent the numbers needed in the next decade): bank loan officers and counselors (99,000), accountants and auditors (330,000), financial managers (297,000), and securities and financial services sales representatives (124,000). Those of you who are interested in these professions should have extensive computer skills. It is also a good idea to take advantage of summer or part-time internship programs, especially in accounting and general business or banking environments, to gain some work experience.

About the Banking Industry

This is a changing industry that has shrunk through numerous mergers and the increasing use of technology. Instead of standing in line at the bank, many convenience-oriented customers now use Automatic Teller Machines (ATMs) to perform electronic transactions—or bank on-line wherever the service is available. This means that banks need fewer tellers and other personnel that support their work.

However, there are still many jobs worth pursuing in this industry. Because of increased competition, banks need marketing-oriented people. They have moved aggressively into the financial markets and need professionals to develop, market, and sell their new and more complex products. Large banks, especially those that have a strong presence in foreign markets, are interested in people with accounting and finance backgrounds to work abroad. One of those markets is Latin America. Back home, however, most banks still offer traditional occupations. One of the most common jobs in commercial banking is that of a lending officer.

Loan Officers and Counselors

When people decide to purchase their first car, or their first home, they must prepare psychologically to part with their hard-earned down payment. They also must trust that the contracts they will sign—and the institution that will lend them money— will not victimize them because they lack experience with these transactions. If the first person who greets them at the bank or credit union, usually a loan officer, speaks their language, that institution has won more than half of the battle to attract them as clients.

The Job

Loan officers work on behalf of institutions that lend money for a variety of purposes. They prepare, analyze, and verify loan applications, decide whether credit should be granted, and help borrowers fill out loan applications. Loan officers usually specialize in one of three types of loans: commercial or business loans, consumer loans (including home equity, automobile, and personal loans), and mortgage loans.

Loan counselors help customers who want to purchase a home or refinance debt, but do not qualify for loans with banks because of their low income or poor credit history. Often, their clients have little or no experience with financial matters and need to be psychologically prepared to become homeowners and to pay their debts.

According to the Bureau of Labor Statistics, loan officers and counselors held about 209,000 jobs in 1996. About six out of ten are employed by commercial banks, savings institutions, and credit unions. Others are employed by financial institutions, such as mortgage brokerage firms and personal credit firms. Most loan counselors work for state and local governments, or for nonprofit organizations. Loan officers and counselors generally work in urban areas where large banks are concentrated.

Education/Training

Most loan officer positions require a bachelor's degree in finance, economics, or a related field. Familiarity with computers and their applications in banking is also expected. Mortgage loan officers are the exception, because they must have training or experience in sales. It is not unusual for loan officers to start out as tellers or customer service representatives and advance through the ranks of their organization as they acquire more work experience.

The American Institute of Banking, which is affiliated with the American Bankers Association, offers courses through correspondence, and in some colleges and universities, for students and others interested in lending, as well as for experienced loan officers. The certification program for lenders leads to the title Certified Lender in Business Banking. Completion of these courses and programs enhances one's employment and advancement opportunities.

Educational requirements for loan counselors vary; some are high school graduates with accounting skills or experience, while others have a college degree in economics, finance, or a related field. Some loan counselors come to their jobs with work experience in a related field. But the majority are provided with intense on-the-job training.

Career Mobility

Loan officers may advance to larger branches of the firm or to managerial positions. Often, the first step is becoming a supervisor over other loan officers and clerical staff. The promotion potential for loan counselors is limited. The most capable can advance to supervisory positions. The best bet is to use the experience as a stepping-stone to other occupations that involve similar functions. These include securities and financial services sales representatives, financial aid officers, real estate agents and brokers, and insurance agents and brokers.

Desired Characteristics

Loan officers and counselors must excel in mathematics, as well as in oral and written communication. Loan officers or counselors have to develop effective working relationships with different people and must enjoy public contact. Often, they are asked to attend community events as representatives of their employer.

Persons interested in counseling should have a strong desire to help others. They must have patience and be trustworthy. They also need an understanding of mortgage banking.

Job Outlook

According to the Bureau of Labor Statistics projections, there will be 99,000 job openings for loan officers and counselors, due to growth and net replacements, between 1996 and 2006. Demand will take place as the population and the economy grow, resulting in increased applications for commercial, consumer, and mortgage loans.

New and varied loan products will add to the demand for experienced loan officers. Because loans are a major source of income for banks, loan officers are considered essential and are less likely to lose their jobs than other workers in banks and other lending institutions during difficult economic times. Also, many loan officers are compensated in part on a commission basis.

Earnings

The form of compensation for loan officers varies, depending on the lending institution. Some banks offer salary plus commission as an incentive to increase the number of loans processed, while others pay only salaries. According to a salary survey conducted by Robert Half International, a staffing services firm specializing in accounting and finance, residential real estate mortgage loan officers earned between $30,600 and $45,000 in 1997; commercial real estate mortgage loan officers earned between $45,100 and $73,000; consumer loan officers, between $28,900 and $48,000; and commercial lenders, between $37,400 and $85,000. Smaller banks generally paid 15 percent less than larger banks. Loan officers who are paid on a commission basis generally earn more than those on salary only.

Banks and other lenders sometimes offer their loan officers free checking privileges and somewhat lower interest rates on personal loans.

The Passion Factor: What do you like most about your occupation?

"It feels great when I drive by a house my customers bought with a loan from our bank," says Mario Rodríguez, a loan officer at a community bank.

With a degree in economics, and an MBA on the way, Rodríguez is poised to move up the career ladder. "I started as a clerk in the audit department," he recalls. "Then I went to night school, thanks to the bank's tuition reimbursement plan."

Related Occupations

Workers who use similar skills are securities and financial services sales representatives, financial aid officers, real estate agents and brokers, and insurance agents and brokers.

Additional Information

American Bankers Association
1120 Connecticut Avenue NW
Washington, DC 20036

Call your state bankers' associations for specific information about job opportunities in your state.

Your local state employment service office or municipal government also may have information on job opportunities, particularly for loan counselors.

Consult one of the following directories for names and addresses of banks and savings and related institutions, as well as the names of their principal officers:

The American Financial Directory (Norcross, GA, McFadden Business Publications).

Polk's World Bank Directory (Nashville, R.L. Polk & Co.).

Rand McNally Bankers Directory (Chicago, Rand McNally & Co.).

The U.S. Savings and Loan Directory (Chicago, Rand McNally & Co.).

Rand McNally Credit Union Directory (Chicago, Rand McNally & Co.).

Accountants and Auditors

"There is definitely a need for Latino accountants," says Ronald Picur, accounting professor and head of that department at the

University of Illinois at Chicago. "Corporate America—particularly the international companies—needs to have a diverse staff to compete in the global market."

The Job

Managers in business, industrial, and government organizations rely on accountants and auditors to prepare, analyze, and verify financial reports and taxes, and monitor information systems. Generally, accountants specialize in one of the four major accounting fields.

Public accountants have their own businesses or work for public accounting firms. They perform a broad range of accounting, auditing, tax, and consulting activities for their clients, who may be corporations, governments, nonprofit organizations, or individuals.

Management accountants, also called **industrial**, **corporate**, or **private accountants**, record and analyze the financial information of the companies for which they work. They also are responsible for budgeting, performance evaluation, cost management, and asset management. They are usually part of executive teams that are involved in strategic planning or new product development.

Government accountants and **auditors** maintain and examine the records of government agencies and audit private businesses and individuals whose activities are subject to government regulations or taxation.

Internal auditors verify the accuracy of their organization's records and check for mismanagement, waste, or fraud.

Within each field, accountants often concentrate on one aspect of accounting. For example, many public accountants concentrate on tax matters, while others concentrate on consulting, and still others specialize in forensic accounting.

Auditors also can be highly specialized. They include electronic data-processing auditors, environmental auditors, engineering auditors, legal auditors, insurance premium auditors, bank auditors, and health care auditors.

At federal, state, and local government levels, accountants verify that revenues are received and expenditures are made in accordance with laws and regulations. Many persons with an accounting background work for the federal government as Internal Revenue Service agents or in financial management, financial institution examination, and budget analysis and administration.

Computers, which are used extensively in accounting and auditing, have taken away some of the tediousness of the manual work associated with figures and records. Some special software packages help accountants summarize transactions in standard formats for financial records or organize data in special formats for financial analysis.

According to the Bureau of Labor Statistics, accountants and auditors held over one million jobs in 1996. Urban areas, where public accounting firms and central or regional offices of businesses are concentrated, attract most accountants and auditors. About 10 percent are self-employed, and a smaller portion work part-time. Some accountants and auditors teach full- or part-time in junior colleges, colleges, and universities.

Education/Training

A bachelor's degree in accounting or a related field is the minimum requirement. But some employers prefer those with a master's degree in accounting or a master's degree in business administration with a concentration in accounting.

Many states will require CPA candidates to complete 150 semester hours of course work prior to taking the CPA exam. By January 1, 2001, at least thirty-two states will have this course work requirement.

In most states, CPAs are the only accountants who are licensed and regulated. Anyone working as a CPA must have a certificate and a license issued by a state board of accountancy. The vast majority of states require CPA candidates to be college graduates, but a few states substitute a certain number of years of public accounting experience for the educational requirement.

Professional societies confer other forms of credentials on a voluntary basis. These include the Certified Management Accountant (CMA) designation given by the Institute of Management Accountants (IMA), the Certified Internal Auditor (CIA) designation by the Institute of Internal Auditors, and the designation of Certified Information Systems Auditor (CISA) by the Information Systems Audit and Control Association.

Career Mobility

Accountants and auditors should advance rapidly. It is possible for graduates of junior colleges and business and correspondence schools, as well as bookkeepers and accounting clerks, to start as junior accountants and advance to more responsible positions as they prove themselves capable of doing the job.

Beginning public accountants usually start by assisting with work for several clients. They may advance to positions with more responsibility in one or two years, and to senior positions within another few years. Those who excel may become supervisors, managers, partners, open their own public accounting firms, or transfer to executive positions in management accounting or internal auditing in private firms.

Most management accountants start as cost accountants, junior internal auditors, or as trainees for other accounting positions. Once they gain experience, they may move up to accounting manager, chief cost accountant, budget director, or manager of internal auditing. Some become controllers, treasurers, financial vice presidents, chief financial officers, or corporation presidents. Many senior corporation executives have a background in accounting, internal auditing, or finance.

Desired Characteristics

Accountants and auditors must have excellent mathematical and analytical skills, and be able to interpret facts and figures quickly to arrive at sound conclusions. Oral and written communication skills are also critical, since accountants and auditors must be able to clearly communicate the results of their work to clients and management.

Accountants and auditors must have good people skills and be able to use and understand business systems and computers. They must be accurate and able to handle responsibility. Above all, accountants and auditors should have high standards of integrity because millions of financial statement users rely on their services.

Job Outlook

According to the Bureau of Labor Statistics, there will be 330,000 jobs for accountants and auditors between 1996 and 2006. More accountants and auditors will be needed to help new businesses set up their books, prepare their taxes, and provide management advice. These businesses, which will grow along with the economy, will later require help with the increased volume and complexity of information developed by accountants and auditors on costs, expenditures, and taxes. Changes in legislation related to taxes, financial reporting standards, business investments, mergers, and other financial matters also will increase the need for accountants and auditors. And, because of the growing international competition, businesses will increasingly need quick, accurate, and individually tailored financial information.

Some growth will occur as a result of the changing role of public accountants, management accountants, and internal auditors. Due to potential liability, public accountants will do less auditing work. And, because of increased competition from tax preparation firms they also will do less tax work. But their role as advisors to management will expand, and so will their consulting services.

Earnings

According to a salary survey conducted by the National Association of Colleges and Employers (NACE), bachelor's degree candidates in accounting received starting offers averaging $29,400 a year in 1996; master's degree candidates in accounting, $33,000.

In a survey of workplaces in 160 metropolitan areas, accountants with limited experience had median earnings of $26,000 in 1995, with the middle half earning between $23,300 and $29,400. The most experienced accountants had median earnings of $87,400, with the middle half earning between $77,600 and $98,000. Public accountants employed by public accounting firms with limited experience had median earnings of $29,400, with the middle half earning between $28,200 and $32,000. The most experienced public accountants had median earnings of $48,700, with the middle half earning between

$44,500 and $54,000. Many owners and partners of firms earned considerably more.

According to a salary survey conducted by Robert Half International, a staffing services firm that specializes in accounting and finance, accountants and auditors with up to one year of experience earned between $25,000 and $39,400 in 1997. Those who had one to three years of experience earned between $27,000 and $46,600. Senior accountants and auditors earned between $34,300 and $57,800; managers earned between $40,000 and $81,900; and directors of accounting and auditing earned between $54,800 and $109,800 a year. The variation in salaries reflects differences in size of firm, location, level of education, and professional credentials.

The Bureau of Labor Statistics reports that in the federal government, the starting annual salary for junior accountants and auditors was about $19,500 in 1997. Candidates who had a superior academic record might start at $24,200, while applicants with a master's degree or two years of professional experience might begin at $29,600. Beginning salaries were slightly higher in selected areas where the prevailing local pay level was higher. Accountants employed by the federal government in nonsupervisory, supervisory, and managerial positions averaged about $54,000 a year in 1997; auditors averaged $57,900.

The Passion Factor: What do you like most about your occupation?

"What I like most about my job is the variety," explains Emilia Díaz referring to her position as an auditor in a mid-sized accounting firm. "Every day I deal with different clients and have the chance to gain many new perspectives."

Born in Mexico, Díaz was always "good with numbers" and excelled in math. But her true love surfaced in high school, when she took her first accounting course. "My teacher really encouraged me," she recalls. Once in the United States, she had to learn to speak English. But her knowledge of accounting proved to be a universal language, allowing her to work in the tax department of a bank until she graduated. Today, she is a bilingual CPA.

Related Occupations

Other workers who use similar skills are appraisers, budget officers, loan officers, financial analysts and managers, bank officers, actuaries, underwriters, tax collectors and revenue agents, FBI special agents, securities sales representatives, and purchasing agents.

Additional Information

> American Association of Hispanic Certified Public
>   Accountants
> 17526 Colima Road, Suite 270
> Rowland Heights, CA 91748
> (818) 965-0643
> http://www.aahcpa.org

> American Institute of Certified Public Accountants
> Harborside Financial Center, 201 Plaza III
> Jersey City, NJ 07311-3881

> Institute of Management Accountants
> 10 Paragon Drive
> Montvale, NJ 07645-1760

> National Society of Public Accountants and the
>   Accreditation Council for Accountancy and Taxation
> 1010 N. Fairfax Street
> Alexandria, VA 22314

Financial Managers

"In the global marketplace, it is helpful to have a second language," says Stephanie DeCicco of the College of Commerce at DePaul University. "It gives [candidates] an edge."

Still, she explains, the key to success in the field of finance is to have a strong background in math and to acquire experience through internships and volunteer jobs.

The Job

Treasurers, **controllers**, **credit managers**, or **cash managers**—the people who prepare the financial reports required by a firm to conduct its operations and to ensure that it satisfies tax and regulatory requirements—are other names for financial managers. Almost every company has at least one. Financial managers also monitor cash flow and the use of financial instruments, control the granting of credit, evaluate risks, raise money, review investments, report on the current and future status of the company, and stay in touch with stockholders and other investors.

Chief financial officers are usually in charge of all financial management functions when the company is small. In large firms, these officers may supervise entire financial management departments where top managers work on the development of financial and economic policies and to establish procedures. In such a setting, each financial department is headed by an experienced financial manager. **Controllers** direct the preparation of all financial reports—income statements, balance sheets, and special reports, such as depreciation schedules. They also oversee the accounting, audit, or budget departments. **Cash** and **credit managers** control cash flow and business investments. **Risk** and **insurance managers** develop programs to reduce risks and losses. **Credit operations managers** set the criteria for credit rating, determine credit ceilings, and monitor their company's credit granting. **Reserve officers** review financial statements and oversee the buying and selling of bonds and other securities to maintain the asset-liability ratio required by law. **User representatives** work in the international accounting arena to create integrated international financial and accounting systems for the banking transactions of multinational organizations. These professionals must have a working knowledge of the financial systems of foreign countries.

The financial managers who work in financial institutions, such as banks, savings and loan associations, and credit unions, may include vice presidents who may be in charge of one or more departments. These include bank branch managers, savings and loan association managers, and credit union managers. Because of the increased domestic and foreign competition, it is essential that financial managers in financial institutions and other corporations be abreast of the ever expanding and complex variety of financial services. Some financial managers in financial institutions may also function as financial planners for individuals and businesses.

According to the Bureau of Labor Statistics, financial managers held about 800,000 jobs in 1996. Approximately one-third work in financial institutions, such as banks, savings institutions, finance companies, credit unions, insurance companies, securities dealers, and real estate firms. Another third are employed by the business, health, social, and management services industries. Nonetheless, financial managers can be found in practically every industry.

Education/Training

Many technically skilled and experienced professionals, such as accountants, budget analysts, credit analysts, insurance analysts, loan officers, and securities analysts, are promoted to financial management positions. At a minimum, financial managers must have a bachelor's degree in accounting or finance, or in business administration with an emphasis on accounting or finance. Increasingly, however, employers seek financial managers with a master's of business administration (MBA).

Financial managers continually need to upgrade their knowledge and skills to be able to function in today's increasingly complex world of global trade, keep up with changing federal and state laws and regulations, and the new financial instruments now available.

Some financial managers may upgrade their skills through professional certification in specialized fields. These include the Association for Investment Management and Research, which confers the Chartered Financial Analyst designation to investment professionals, and the National Association of Credit Management which offers a three-part certification program for business credit professionals.

Career Mobility

Because of their key position within a company, financial managers who have experience, proven ability and leadership qualities, and who can show that they truly understand how various departments operate, are the most likely to be promoted to top management positions. More experienced managers may open their own consulting firms.

Desired Characteristics

Financial managers have to like working independently, and analyzing detailed information. They must be thoroughly familiar with the applications of computer technology to the field of finance. In addition, they should be effective communicators with excellent people skills to establish productive personal relationships with the staff they supervise.

Job Outlook

According to the Bureau of Labor Statistics, there will be 297,000 job openings for financial managers between 1996 and 2006, due to growth and net replacements. The increase in global trade and availability of sophisticated financial instruments, as well as the changes in federal and state laws and regulations, will spur the demand for skilled financial managers. Best prospects may be in rapidly growing industries such as health care.

Earnings

The Bureau of Labor Statistics reports that the median annual salary of financial managers was $40,700 in 1996. The lowest 10 percent earned $21,800 or less, while the top 10 percent earned over $81,100.

According to a 1997 survey done by staffing services firm Robert Half International, salaries of assistant controllers range from $41,000 in the smallest firms to $81,000 in the largest firms; those of controllers, $47,000 to $138,000. Salaries of chief financial officers/treasurers range from $62,000 to $307,000.

The results of the Treasury Management Association's 1997 compensation survey are presented in the table on the next page. The earnings listed here represent total compensation, including bonuses. The survey also found that financial managers with a master's degree in business administration average $10,900 more than managers with a bachelor's degree.

Annual Earnings for Selected Financial Managers, 1997

Chief financial officer	$142,900
Vice president of finance	138,000
Treasurer	122,500
Assistant treasurer	88,400
Controller	85,100
Treasury manager	66,900
Assistant controller	56,200
Senior analyst	55,600
Cash manager	51,600
Analyst	40,500
Assistant cash manager	38,800

Source: Treasury Management Association

Salary level also depends upon the manager's experience and the size and location of the organization. It is likely to be higher in larger organizations and cities. Many financial managers in private industry receive additional compensation in the form of bonuses, which also vary substantially by the size of the firm.

The Passion Factor: What do you like most about your occupation?

"I love to see our customers buying the bank's financial products," says Estela Sánchez, branch manager of a mid-sized bank.

Starting out at a community college, she was exposed to accounting for the first time and liked it. "Then I went to work for a manufacturing company that had tuition reimbursement benefits," she continued. Sánchez went on to get a bachelor's degree in finance, and later an MBA.

Related Occupations

Other professionals who may use similar skills are accountants and auditors, budget officers, credit analysts, loan officers, insurance consultants, portfolio managers, pension consultants, real estate advisors, securities analysts, and underwriters.

Additional Information

American Bankers Association
Center for Banking Information
1120 Connecticut Avenue NW
Washington, DC 20036

National Association of Credit Management (NACM)
Credit Research Foundation
8815 Centre Park Drive
Columbia, MD 21045-2117

Treasury Management Association
7315 Wisconsin Avenue
Bethesda, MD 20814

Association for Investment Management and Research
5 Boar's Head Lane, PO Box 3668
Charlottesville, VA 22903

Healthcare Financial Management Association
Two Westbrook Corporate Center, Suite 700
Westchester, IL 60154

National Society of Hispanic MBAs
PO Box 224747
1110 Browder
Dallas, TX 75222
(214) 428-1622

Securities and Financial Services Sales Representatives

Bucking most other trends, this particular profession favors more mature individuals who have extensive sales experience. If you are young and interested in tapping the Latino market through this arena, seek a broker or financial planner who might be willing to become your mentor. "Shadow" this person as much as possible and watch for those behaviors that make him or her successful in this business.

The Job

Securities sales representatives, also called **stockbrokers**, **account executives**, or **registered representatives**, are the professionals who buy or sell stocks, bonds, shares in mutual funds, insurance annuities, or other financial products for individual and corporate investors.

From their offices, sales representatives may communicate a customer's order to the floor of a securities exchange, such as the New York Stock Exchange, where a securities sales representative, known as a brokers' floor representative, can buy and sell securities.

Based on their customers' needs, securities sales representatives may also provide them with many related services. For example, they may prepare a financial portfolio which could include life insurance, corporate and municipal bonds, securities, mutual funds, certificates of deposit, and annuities. Sometimes, they may have to explain the meaning of stock market terms and trading practices, or offer financial counseling.

Securities sales representatives find out what investment goals their customers have, so they can explain the advantages and disadvantages of a particular investment based on each person's objectives. Some people may want long-term, conservative investments while others might prefer speculative securities where the value may increase rapidly but the risk is greater. If the investor is interested in a particular security, the sales representative can give him up-to-date price quotations, along with information on the activities and financial positions of the corporations issuing these securities.

Some securities sales representatives specialize in institutional investing, where they concentrate on specific financial products such as annuities, options, stocks, bonds, or commodity futures. Some also handle the sale of new issues.

Perhaps the biggest challenge for a sales representative is to find clients and build a customer base. Some meet clients by networking over the phone or at social or professional events, while others offer investment workshops, seminars, or classes at libraries or community colleges to gain more exposure.

The majority of securities sales representatives work for a small number of large firms with main offices in large cities, especially New York. Others are employed by relatively small brokerage and investment firms in all parts of the country.

Financial services sales representatives sell banking services such as certificates of deposit, lines of credit, deposit accounts, inventory financing, cash management, or investment services. The role of these professionals has gained importance since banks became competitive through the sale of complex financial services, such as securities brokerage and financial planning. In small and medium-size banks, branch managers and commercial loan officers are the ones who usually market the bank's financial services.

Financial services sales representatives usually work for banks, savings and loan associations, or other credit institutions.

Financial planners analyze their clients' assets, liabilities, cash flow, insurance coverage, tax status, and financial objectives to develop and implement a financial plan tailored to their needs. To accomplish this, financial planners rely on their knowledge of tax and investment strategies, securities, pension plans, real estate, and insurance. Usually, they work as sole practitioners or in small firms.

Education/Training

Even though employers rarely demand specialized academic training, the vast majority of securities sales representatives are college graduates. Because they must be well aware of economic conditions and trends, courses in business administration, economics, and finance are useful in this profession. Training in the use of computers is important, as the securities sales business is highly automated.

Securities sales representatives must meet state licensing requirements, which generally include passing an examination and, in some cases, furnishing a personal bond. In addition, sales representatives must register as representatives of their firm according to regulations of the securities exchanges where they do business or the National Association of Securities Dealers, Inc. (NASD). Before beginners can qualify as registered representatives, they must pass the General Securities Registered Representative Examination, administered by the NASD, and be an employee of a registered firm for at least four months. Most states also require a second examination.

Many securities sales representatives take correspondence courses in preparation for the securities examinations. However, most employers provide on-the-job training to help securities sales representatives meet the requirements for registration. In most firms, the training period generally takes about four months. Large firms may offer their trainees classroom instruction in securities analysis, effective speaking, and sales; or they may take courses offered by business schools and associations; and undergo a period of on-the-job training lasting up to two years. Many firms like to rotate their trainees among various departments in the firm to give them a broader perspective of the securities business. In small firms, sales representatives generally receive training in outside institutions and on the job.

To work in banks or other credit institutions, financial services sales representatives need a business administration degree with a concentration in finance or a liberal arts degree. Courses in accounting, economics, and marketing provide a good foundation for this job. Financial services sales representatives learn through on-the-job training under the supervision of bank officers.

Career Mobility

Securities sales representatives usually advance in their profession by increasing the number and size of the accounts they handle. In time, those beginners who serviced the accounts of individual investors may handle large institutional accounts such as those of banks and pension funds. With experience, some sales representatives become branch office managers and supervise other sales representatives while continuing to provide services for their own customers. A few representatives advance to top management positions or become partners in their firms. Financial services sales representatives can be promoted to managerial positions if their performance is outstanding.

Desired Characteristics

Sales ability and good communication skills, as well as self-confidence and an ability to handle frequent rejections, are key ingredients for success in this occupation. Maturity and the ability to work independently also are important. People with on-commission sales experience, particularly those who have worked in real estate or insurance, can make excellent securities sales representatives.

Job Outlook

The Bureau of Labor Statistics estimates that there will be 124,000 openings for securities and financial sales workers between 1996 and 2006, due to growth and net replacements. Economic growth, rising personal incomes, and greater inherited wealth increase the funds available for investment, thus creating demand for these professionals. As more individual investors purchase common stocks, mutual funds, and other financial products, they will need the advice of securities sales representatives regarding the increasing array of investment alternatives.

The number and size of institutional investors is also expected to grow as more people enroll in pension plans, set up individual retirement accounts, establish trust funds, and contribute to the endowment funds of colleges and other nonprofit institutions.

More representatives also will be needed to sell securities issued by new and expanding corporations, by state and local governments financing public improvements, and by foreign governments, whose securities have become attractive to U.S. investors as international trade expands.

The future also looks promising for the growing number of financial planners as investors increasingly rely on them for help in selecting the appropriate options among a wide variety of financial alternatives. In addition, demand should increase as banks and credit institutions expand the range of financial services they offer and issue more loans for personal and commercial use.

Earnings

According to the Bureau of Labor Statistics, median annual earnings of securities and financial services sales representatives were $38,800 in 1996; the middle 50 percent earned between $24,300 and $73,500. Ten percent earned less than $18,100 and 10 percent earned more than $98,400. On average, financial services sales representatives earn considerably less than securities sales representatives.

Until trainees are licensed and registered, they usually are paid a salary. Thereafter, their earnings depend on commissions from the sale or purchase of stocks and bonds, life insurance, or other securities for customers. Commission earnings are likely to be high when there is much buying and selling and lower when there is a slump in market activity. Most firms provide sales representatives with a steady income by paying a "draw against commission"—that is, a minimum salary based on the commissions which they can be expected to earn. Securities sales representatives who can provide their clients with the most complete financial services should enjoy the greatest income stability.

Financial services sales representatives usually are paid a salary; some receive a bonus if they meet certain established goals.

The Passion Factor: What do you like most about your occupation?

"There is a very special feeling that comes from making money for your clients," reports María Escalante, a portfolio manager who owns an asset management company.

Born in Colombia, she always had "an independent mind and a nose for a good deal." Maybe that's why she became a successful entrepreneur who makes her living helping others become wealthy.

Related Occupations

Other workers who need similar skills are insurance agents and real estate agents.

Additional Information

Contact individual securities firms and/or state bankers' associations to inquire about job openings.

Technology Careers

Technology is at the root of the revolutionary changes we have witnessed over the last few years. It has transformed the way we live and work. We now have gadgets our parents never imagined could exist, from the alarm clock that lets you snooze without fear of oversleeping to the car that "remembers" how far you like the driver's seat to recline, to the satellites that send us pictures from Mars. And, thanks to the computer and its related communication tools, we can telecommute instead of taking the train or driving to the office. Beyond our daily endeavors, technology has made it possible for us to instantly reach people across the globe—whether via fax, e-mail, phone or teleconferencing—thus bringing us closer to other cultures and to very different points of view.

There are people and jobs behind all this innovation. While technology has been blamed for jobs lost, it also continuously creates new occupations (such as the still-evolving web-related professions) or modifies existing ones (for example, a graphic designer can perform his work on a computer screen as well as on paper). The following example will serve to illustrate some of the demand and dilemmas high technology has created.

Web sites are becoming increasingly important to businesses around the world. They not only provide an additional and very powerful vehicle to sell products, they also offer an opportunity to put the best face on a company. In other words, web sites also have become a public relations tool. For most colleges and universities, for example, a web site is now an invaluable and incredibly fast medium to attract new students. The expense of mailing college catalogs is cut down considerably (because mailings can be more targeted), and the waiting time between browsing and making the decision to apply is also reduced.

Because these sites have acquired such significance, the job requirements for a webmaster—still quite a new occupation—have changed considerably already. Every technological advance related to the Internet calls for additional skills. And each time someone finds another way to utilize the Internet, more workers (with different skill sets) are needed to accomplish the task. For example, companies now want the webmaster to know what their business is about. This means that they expect the webmaster to have some business acumen, in addition to the technical skills which are now becoming widespread. And that he or she will have or need to hire expertise in graphic design, writing, public relations, and advertising. Finally, the webmaster needs to keep the team and the web site working smoothly.

Latinos are poised to take advantage of many of these new opportunities. If world borders are said to be figuratively blurring, they are nonexistent on the Internet. Already, it is possible to find a variety of U.S. sites in Spanish, plus those which can be reached in other countries. And the Spanish-speaking world needs people to help bring it technologically up to par.

To get there, you can delve into some yet unexplored areas related to computers through recently established professions. Or, you can choose more traditional routes (such as engineering). Both are likely to yield excellent results.

Information Technology

Jobs in Information Technology (IT) are still evolving. They are too fluid and new for anyone to look into the future and predict "how many of each" we will need. A number of concerned organizations and businesses, including the Microsoft Corporation, have been working to develop job titles along with skill standards required to perform each of those jobs. In addition to the more established jobs of **computer analysts** and **technical writers**, they include **multimedia specialists**, **interactive digital media specialists** and **technical support representatives**. The want ads also mention **Internet specialists**, **Internet managers**, and **regional Internet account managers**.

Regardless of their title or job requirements, the consensus is that these occupations will continue to grow at a very fast pace, and that there is a severe shortage of skilled workers to fulfill them even now. According to a recent study conducted by the Information Technology Association of America, one in ten (or 346,000) IT job openings in U.S. companies remained vacant in 1997.

The field is wide open then. But before you choose it, remember that in information technology, perhaps more than in any other discipline, only those who can stay ahead of its constantly evolving knowledge base will succeed.

Computer Scientists and Systems Analysts

The proliferation of computers and computer-based technology has spawned the need for highly skilled professionals who can design and develop computer hardware and software systems and integrate them with new or existing systems. While this occupational category encompasses a variety of jobs whose titles are not used uniformly, most fall under the umbrella of computer and data processing services. This industry is expected to more than double its employment size to 2.5 million workers by 2006. It has the three fastest growing occupations: database administrators, computer support specialists, and all other computer scientists; computer engineers; and systems analysts. This section will describe those occupations along with their expected opportunities.

The Job

Computer scientists design computers and develop and adapt principles for applying computers to new uses. Their work is highly theoretical and involves the creation or application of new technology. Computer scientists include **computer engineers**, **database administrators**, **computer support analysts**, and a variety of other specialized workers.

Those professionals who work in academic institutions may be involved with theory, hardware, or language design. Some work on multidisciplinary projects, for example, developing and advancing uses for virtual reality. In private industry, computer scientists may develop specialized languages, or design programming tools, knowledge-based systems, or computer games.

Computer engineers work with the hardware and software aspects of systems design and development. Software engineers design and develop both packaged and systems software.

Database administrators work with database management systems software. They also may be responsible for maintaining the efficiency of the database, and the system security.

Computer support analysts help users to interpret problems and provide them with technical support for hardware, software, and systems. They may work within an organization or directly for the computer or software vendor.

Systems analysts study business, scientific, or engineering data processing problems and design new solutions using computers. They may design entirely new systems, including both hardware and software, or add a single new software application to harness more of the computer's power. Their objective is to help an organization realize the maximum benefit from its investment in equipment, personnel, and business processes.

Analysts normally begin an assignment by conducting a needs-assessment with managers and users. After clearly defining the goals of the system, they may use techniques such as structured analysis, data modeling, information engineering, mathematical model-building, sampling, and cost accounting to plan the system. Analysts must specify the files and records the system will access, and design the processing steps as well as the format for the output that will meet the users' needs. Once the design is developed, systems analysts prepare charts and diagrams to describe it in terms that managers and other users can understand. They may prepare a cost-benefit and return-on-investment analysis to help management decide whether the proposed system will be satisfactory and financially feasible.

When a system is accepted, the analysts may determine what computer hardware and software will be needed to set it up or make changes. They coordinate testing of the system to ensure it performs as planned. They prepare specifications, work diagrams, and structure charts for computer programmers to follow and then work with them to "debug," or eliminate errors from the system. Some organizations do not employ programmers; instead, a single worker called a programmer-analyst is responsible for both systems analysis and programming.

Many systems analysts are involved with "networking" all the computers in an individual office, department, or establishment. This has many variations and may be referred to as local area networks (LAN), wide area networks, or multi-user systems. A primary goal of networking is to allow personal computer (PC) users to access data from a mainframe computer and use it on their machine. This connection also allows data to be entered into the mainframe from the PC.

Systems analysts also may be involved in making the computer systems in each department compatible so that up-to-date information, such as accounting records, sales figures, or budget projections, can be shared. Similarly, electronic mail requires open pathways to send messages, documents, and data from one computer "mailbox" to another across different equipment and program lines. Analysts must design the gates in the hardware and software to allow free exchange of data, custom applications, and the computer power to process it all. They study the seemingly incompatible pieces and create ways to link them so that users can access information from any part of the system.

According to the Bureau of Labor Statistics, computer scientists, computer engineers, and systems analysts held about 933,000 jobs in 1996, including about 58,000 who were self-employed. About 216,000 were computer engineers; about 506,000 were computer systems analysts; and about 212,000 were database administrators, computer support specialists, and all other computer scientists.

Although computer scientists and systems analysts work in just about any industry, the great majority are employed in the computer and data processing services industry. This includes firms that design and install computer systems; integrate or network systems; perform data processing and database management; develop packaged software; and even operate entire computer facilities under contract. Many others work for government agencies, manufacturers of computer and related electronic equipment, insurance companies, and universities.

A growing number of computer scientists and systems analysts are employed on a temporary or contract basis, or as consultants. Given the technology available today, more work, including technical support, can be done from remote locations with the use of modems, laptops, electronic mail, and even through the Internet.

Education/Training

Although there is no universally accepted path to become a computer professional, employers almost always seek college graduates for those positions. Generally, computer scientist jobs in research laboratories or academic institutions require a PhD, or at least a master's degree in computer science or engineering. Computer engineers generally require a bachelor's degree in computer engineering, electrical engineering, or math. Computer support analysts may also need a bachelor's degree in a computer-related field, as well as significant experience working with computers, including programming skills.

Many employers seek candidates with a bachelor's degree in computer science, information science, computer information systems, or data processing for systems analyst or even database administrator positions.

The Institute for Certification of Computing Professionals offers the designation Certified Computing Professional (CCP) to those who have at least four years of work experience as a computer professional, or at least two years experience and a college degree. The Quality Assurance Institute awards the designation Certified Quality Analyst (CQA) to those who meet education and experience requirements, pass an exam, and endorse a code of ethics. Neither designation is mandatory.

Career Mobility

After several years of experience, systems analysts may be promoted to senior or lead systems analysts. Those with leadership ability also can advance to management positions, such as manager of information systems or chief information officer.

Computer engineers and scientists employed in industry may eventually advance into managerial or project leadership positions. Those employed in academic institutions can become heads of research departments or published authorities in their field. Computer professionals with several years of experience and considerable expertise in a particular area may choose to start their own computer consulting firms.

Desired Characteristics

Prior work experience is very important. Some people, who may not have a computer-related degree, develop advanced computer skills in other occupations and then transfer into computer occupations.

These professionals must be familiar with programming languages and have broad knowledge of and experience with computer systems and technologies. A background in business management or a closely related field is expected for jobs in a business environment. Scientifically oriented organizations, on the other hand, want systems analysts with a background in the physical sciences, applied mathematics, or engineering.

Systems analysts must be able to think logically, have good communication skills, and like working with ideas and people. They must be able to deal with a number of tasks simultaneously, but still pay close attention to detail. Both computer scientists and systems analysts often work in teams on large projects. They need to communicate effectively with computer personnel, such as programmers and managers, as well as with other staff who have no technical computer background. Employers will increasingly seek computer professionals who can combine strong programming and traditional systems analysis skills with good interpersonal and business skills.

Job Outlook

The Bureau of Labor Statistics projects that there will be 1,072,000 job openings for computer systems analysts, engineers, and scientists between 1996 and 2006, due to growth and net replacements. Employment growth will be driven by several factors. Competition pressures will force organizations to maximize the efficiency of their computer systems. There will continue to be a need for increasingly sophisticated technological innovation in areas such as office and factory automation, telecommunications technology, and scientific research. As the complexity of these applications grows, more computer scientists and systems analysts will be needed to design, develop, and implement the new technology.

As more computing power is made available to the individual user, more computer scientists and systems analysts will be required to provide support.

The demand for "networking" to facilitate the sharing of information will be a major factor in the rising demand for systems analysts. Falling prices of computer hardware and software should continue to induce more small businesses to computerize their operations, further stimulating demand for these workers. To remain competitive, these businesses will need the continued services of systems analysts.

Earnings

According to the Bureau of Labor Statistics, median annual earnings of computer systems analysts and scientists who worked full time in 1996 were about $46,300. The middle 50 percent earned between $34,000 and $59,900. The lowest 10 percent earned less than $24,800 and the highest tenth, more than $76,200. Computer scientists with advanced degrees generally earn more than systems analysts.

Starting salaries for computer scientists or computer engineers with a bachelor's degree can be significantly higher than starting salaries of bachelor's degree graduates in many other fields. According to the National Association of Colleges and Employers, starting salary offers for graduates with a bachelor's degree in computer engineering averaged about $39,722 a year in 1997; those with a master's degree, $44,734 a year; and those with a PhD, $63,367. Starting offers for graduates with a bachelor's degree in computer science averaged about $36,597 a year; in information sciences, about $35,407 a year; and in systems analysis, about $43,800 a year in 1997. Offers for those with the bachelor's degree vary by functional area for all types of employers, as shown below.

Offers for graduates with a master's degree in computer science in 1997 averaged $45,853 a year, and those with a PhD in computer and information sciences, $61,306.

According to Robert Half International, starting salaries in 1997 for systems analysts employed by large establishments employing more than fifty staff members ranged from $46,000 to

Average Starting Salaries for Selected Computer-Related Specialists with Bachelors' Degrees, 1997

Computer programming	$35,167
Information systems	34,689
Systems analysis and design	36,261
Software design and development	39,190
Hardware design and development	41,237

Source: National Association of Colleges and Employers

$57,500. Salaries for those employed in small establishments ranged from $38,000 to $48,000. Salaries for programmer-analysts ranged from $39,000 to $50,000 in large establishments and $33,500 to $43,000 in small establishments. Starting salaries ranged from $54,000 to $67,500 for database administrators, from $36,000 to $55,000 for network administrators, from $25,000 to $36,500 for help desk support technicians, and from $49,000 to $67,500 for software development specialists.

In the federal government, the entrance salary for systems analysts who are recent college graduates with a bachelor's degree was about $19,520 a year in early 1997; for those with a superior academic record, $24,180. The average annual salary for computer engineers in the federal government in nonsupervisory, supervisory, and managerial positions was $62,900 in early 1997.

The Passion Factor: What do you like most about your occupation?

"I am passionate about my profession," says Carlos Alcorta, a senior systems analyst who works for a management consulting firm. "There are always problems to be solved, each representing a new situation, and each requiring creativity and experience to bring about a solution."

Born in Peru, Alcorta has two master's degrees, one in computer engineering and the other in business administration. As a consultant, he often works in different parts of the country, such as Boston and Detroit, and, because he is also bicultural and bilingual, he has been offered a short-term assignment in Spain.

Related Occupations

Other professionals whose occupation requires similar skills are computer programmers, financial analysts, urban planners, engineers, operations research analysts, management analysts, and actuaries.

Additional Information

Association for Computing Machinery
1515 Broadway
New York, NY 10036

Institute for the Certification of Computing Professionals
2200 E. Devon Avenue, Suite 268
Des Plaines, IL 60018

Quality Assurance Institute
7575 Dr. Phillips Boulevard, Suite 350
Orlando, FL 32819

Computer Programmers

The Job

Computer programmers write and maintain the detailed instructions, called programs or software, that list in a logical order the steps that computers must execute to perform their functions. They then code these instructions in a conventional programming language, such as C and FORTRAN, or one of the more advanced artificial intelligence or object oriented languages, such as LISP, Prolog, C++, or Ada. Sometimes, programmers follow descriptions prepared by systems analysts. In smaller organizations, **programmer-analysts** are responsible for both systems analysis and programming.

Although simple programs can be written in a few hours, programs that use complex mathematical formulas or many data files may require more than a year of work. In most cases, several programmers may work together as a team under a senior programmer's supervision.

Programmers in software development companies may work directly with experts from various fields to create software ranging from games and educational software to programs for desktop publishing, financial planning, and spreadsheets. Much of the programming being done today is the preparation of packaged software, one of the most rapidly growing segments of the computer industry. Still, many programmers are involved in updating, repairing, and modifying code for existing programs.

When a program is ready to be tested, programmers do trial runs and review the results. If errors occur, the appropriate changes are made and the program is rechecked until it produces the correct results. This is called "debugging" the program.

Programmers who work in a mainframe environment prepare instructions for the computer operator who will run the program.

Generally, there are two broad types of programmers: **applications** and **systems programmers**.

Applications programmers tend to be business, engineering, or science oriented. The software they write handles specific jobs (such as a program used in an inventory control system).

Systems programmers maintain the software that controls the operation of an entire computer system. These professionals make changes in the instructions that determine how the system's central processing unit handles the various jobs it has been given and how it communicates with peripheral equipment, such as terminals, printers, and disk drives. Because of their knowledge of the entire computer system, systems programmers often help applications programmers determine the source of problems that may occur with their programs.

According to the Bureau of Labor Statistics, computer programmers held about 568,000 jobs in 1996. While they can work in any industry, the vast majority are employed in data processing service organizations, including firms that write and sell software; firms that provide engineering and management services; manufacturers of computer and office equipment; financial institutions; insurance carriers; educational institutions; and government agencies.

Applications programmers work for all types of firms, whereas systems programmers usually work for organizations with large computer centers or for firms that manufacture computers or develop software. A growing number of programmers are employed on a temporary or contract basis.

Education/Training

Computer programming is taught at most public and private vocational schools, community and junior colleges, and universities. However, the field has become much more competitive due to the large number of available qualified applicants and the increasing complexity of some programming tasks. Although some programmers obtain two-year degrees or certificates, bachelor's degrees are now more commonly required.

The majority of programmers hold a four-year degree. Of these, some hold a BA or BS in computer science or information systems, while others have taken special courses in computer programming to supplement their study in fields such as accounting, inventory control, or other business areas.

College graduates with degrees in computer or information science, mathematics, engineering, or the physical sciences are preferred by employers who use computers for scientific or engineering applications. Some jobs require graduate degrees. Employers who use computers for business applications prefer to hire people who have had college courses in management information systems (MIS) and business, and who possess strong programming skills.

Career Mobility

In large organizations, skilled workers may be promoted to lead programmer and be afforded some supervisory responsibilities. Some applications programmers may move into systems programming after they gain experience and take courses in systems software.

With general business experience, both applications programmers and systems programmers may become systems analysts or be promoted to a managerial position. Other programmers with specialized knowledge and experience with a language or operating system may work in research and development areas such as multimedia or Internet technology. As employers increasingly contract out programming jobs, more opportunities should arise for experienced programmers with expertise in a specific area to work as consultants.

Desired Characteristics

Industries need computer programmers who have programming skills, can think logically, and pay close attention to detail. Patience, persistence, and the ability to work on exacting analytical work, especially under pressure, are a plus. Ingenuity and imagination are needed to help find solutions, and interpersonal skills to work in teams and interact directly with users.

Systems programmers must have the ability to work with abstract concepts and do technical analysis because they work with the software that controls the computer's operation.

Job Outlook

The Bureau of Labor Statistics estimates that there will be 306,000 job openings for computer programmers between 1996 and 2006, due to growth and net replacements. Jobs for systems and applications programmers will continue to be particularly abundant in data processing service firms, software houses, and computer consulting businesses. These types of establishments remain part of one of the fastest growing industries—computer and data processing services. Companies needing to control costs will look to this industry to meet their programming needs.

As organizations seek new applications for computers and improvements to the software already in use, the demand for skilled programmers will increase. Employers are increasingly interested in programmers who can combine areas of technical expertise or who are adaptable and able to learn and incorporate new skills. Progress will expand opportunity in data communications and networking computers. Object-oriented languages will increasingly be used in the years ahead, further enhancing the productivity of programmers. Programmers will be creating and maintaining expert systems and embedding these technologies in more and more products.

Earnings

According to the National Association of Colleges and Employers, median earnings of programmers who worked full-time in 1996 were about $40,100 a year. The middle 50 percent earned between $30,700 and $52,000 a year. The lowest 10 percent earned less than $22,700; the highest 10 percent earned more than $65,200. Starting salary offers for graduates with a bachelor's degree in the area of computer programming averaged about $35,167 a year in private industry in 1997. Programmers working in the West and Northeast earned somewhat more than those working in the South and Midwest. On average, systems programmers earn more than applications programmers.

A survey of workplaces in 160 metropolitan areas found that beginning programmers had median annual earnings of about $27,000 in 1995. Experienced mid-level programmers with some supervisory responsibilities had median annual earnings of about $40,000. Median annual earnings for programmers at the supervisory or team leader level were about $55,000.

The Passion Factor: What do you like most about your occupation?

"Solving problems as a team is what I like the most," says Esteban Catalano, a programmer analyst working for a small manufacturing concern.

"I always liked math and figuring things out. I guess I was destined to love what I do."

Related Occupations

Other professionals whose occupation requires similar skills are statisticians, engineers, financial analysts, accountants and auditors, actuaries, and operations research analysts.

Additional Information

Contact your state employment service offices for information about jobs for computer programmers. Also check with your city's chamber of commerce for information on the area's largest employers.

For information about certification as a computing professional, see *Additional Information* under Computer Scientists and Systems Analysts.

The More Traditional Technologies

The Bureau of Labor Statistics projects that there will be 580,000 job openings for engineers, with three branches—electrical and electronic, civil, and mechanical—getting the lion's share of those jobs. Following are their descriptions.

Engineering

The Job

Utilizing their knowledge of mathematics and science, engineers devise practical applications for existing or newly discovered technology. They may design products such as CD players and coffee-makers, machines such as dishwashers or tractors, and systems and processes for creating, modifying, or maintaining a product that can function efficiently and economically. Some may design defense-related goods or weapons systems for the armed forces, while others will be involved in designing, planning, and supervising the construction of buildings, highways, and rapid transit systems. Their designs also may include systems for control and automation of manufacturing, business, and management processes.

Because their objective is to create a product with practical applications, engineers usually approach a design by determining the exact function it is expected to perform, so they can design and test components and fit them together in an integrated plan. As a last step, they evaluate the design to test its effectiveness, cost, reliability, and safety. This process applies to products as different as chemicals, computers, gas turbines, helicopters, and toys.

Some engineers' work may entail testing manufactured products to maintain quality. Others may supervise production in factories to determine the causes of breakdowns, and estimate the time and cost to complete projects. Some work in engineering management or in sales.

The vast majority of engineers specialize. Professional societies recognize more than twenty-five major specialties, and there are numerous subdivisions within the major branches. Structural, environmental, and transportation engineering, for example, are subdivisions of civil engineering. Some areas of specialization are aerospace, architecture, biomedicine, chemicals, civil-construction, electricity and electronics, environment, industry, mechanics, materials, mining, nuclear energy, and petroleum products. Engineers also may specialize within one industry, or in one field of technology.

Engineers use computers extensively—sometimes to simulate and test how a machine, structure, or system operates, and others to take advantage of computer-aided design (CAD) systems to produce and analyze designs. When complex projects require it, they work with an interdisciplinary team of engineers.

According to the Bureau of Labor Statistics, engineers held 1,382,000 jobs in 1996. Forty-seven percent of all engineers work in manufacturing industries, primarily in electrical and electronic equipment, industrial machinery, scientific instruments, aircraft and parts, motor vehicles, chemicals, guided missiles and space vehicles, fabricated metal products, and primary metals industries.

Those working in nonmanufacturing industries are concentrated in engineering and architectural services, research and testing services, and business services. Engineers also work in the communications, utilities, and construction industries.

Engineers also are employed by federal, state, and local governments. At the federal level, they work mainly in the Departments of Defense, Transportation, Agriculture, Interior, and Energy, and at the National Aeronautics and Space Administration (NASA). In state and local government agencies, they usually work in highway and public works departments. Some engineers are self-employed consultants.

Education/Training

A bachelor's degree in engineering is usually the minimum education required for beginning engineering jobs. Occasionally, college graduates with a degree in a physical science or mathematics may qualify for some engineering jobs, especially in engineering specialties in high demand.

The majority of engineering degrees are granted in the electrical, mechanical, or civil branches. However, engineers trained in one branch have the flexibility to work in another—a real advantage when engineers are in short supply in certain specialties, or when employment prospects are better in other fields.

Many colleges also offer degrees in engineering technology (as either two- or four-year programs) to prepare students for more practical design and production work than the traditional theoretical and scientifically oriented jobs.

Although there are approximately 340 colleges and universities offering bachelor's degrees in engineering, and another 300 colleges offering bachelor's degrees in engineering technology, all are not accredited programs. Some emphasize one type of practice over another and a very few offer concentrations in the smaller specialties. Check course descriptions and ask questions before sending in your application.

Typically, engineering programs are four years long. However, many students take up to five years to complete them. Some programs offer a general engineering curriculum and students then specialize in graduate school or on the job.

Graduate training is essential for engineering faculty positions but is not required for the majority of entry-level engineering jobs. Many engineers obtain graduate degrees in engineering or business administration to learn new technology, broaden their education, and enhance promotion opportunities. Many high-level executives in government and industry began their careers as engineers.

Some colleges and universities offer five-year master's degree programs. Some five- or even six-year cooperative plans combine classroom study and practical work, permitting students to gain valuable experience and finance part of their education.

All fifty states and the District of Columbia require registration for engineers whose work may affect life, health, or property, or who offer their services to the public.

Career Mobility

Engineers may become technical specialists or may supervise a staff or team of engineers and technicians. Some eventually become engineering managers or enter other managerial, management support, or sales jobs.

Engineers must continue their education throughout their careers because much of their value to their employer depends on their knowledge of the latest technology. The pace of technological change varies by engineering specialty and industry. Engineers in high-technology areas such as advanced electronics may find that technical knowledge can become obsolete rapidly. Even those who continue their education are vulnerable if the particular technology or product they have specialized in becomes obsolete. Engineers who have not kept current in their field may find themselves passed over for promotions and vulnerable should layoffs occur. On the other hand, it is often these high-technology areas that offer the greatest challenges, the most interesting work, and the highest salaries. Therefore, the choice of engineering specialty and employer involves an assessment not only of the potential rewards but also of the risk of technological obsolescence.

Desired Characteristics

Engineers should be creative, analytical, and detail-oriented. They must be able to communicate well—both orally and in writing—and be able to work as part of a team.

Engineers also need a solid background in mathematics (algebra, geometry, trigonometry, and calculus), science (biology, chemistry, and physics), and courses in English, social studies, humanities, and computers.

Job Outlook

According to the Bureau of Labor Statistics, there will be 580,000 job openings for engineers through the year 2006, due to growth and net replacements. The best opportunities will be in electrical and electronic engineering, followed by civil and mechanical engineering. Growth in employment will be driven by intense global and domestic competition, along with new technology. Competition will force companies to improve and update product designs more frequently. Also, employers who invest in plant facilities and equipment to expand their production of goods and services will rely on engineers to improve productivity. More engineers will be needed to improve or replace deteriorating roads, bridges, water and pollution control systems, and other aging public facilities.

Freshman engineering enrollments began to decline in 1983, and thus the number of bachelor's degrees in engineering began declining in 1987. This decline is expected to continue through the late 1990s, partly because the total college-age population is projected to decline.

Only a relatively small proportion of engineers leave the profession each year. Nonetheless, more than 70 percent of all job openings will occur as a result of replacement needs. A greater proportion of replacement openings is created by engineers who transfer to management, sales, or other professional specialty occupations than by those who leave the labor force.

Earnings

Starting salaries for engineers with a bachelor's degree are significantly higher than starting salaries of bachelor's degree graduates in other fields. According to the National Association of Colleges and Employers, engineering graduates with a bachelor's degree averaged about $38,500 a year in private industry in 1997; those with a master's degree and no experience, $45,400 a year; and those with a PhD, $59,200. Starting salaries for those

Average Starting Salaries for Engineering Graduates with a Bachelor's Degree, by Branch

Engineering Field	Starting Annual Wages
Aerospace	$37,957
Chemical	42,817
Civil	33,119
Electrical	39,513
Industrial	38,026
Mechanical	38,113
Petroleum	43,674

Source: National Association of Colleges and Employers

Median Annual Salaries for Selected Engineering Specialties

Aerospace	$57,000
Chemical	52,600
Civil	46,000
Electrical	51,700
Industrial	43,700
Mechanical	49,700

Source: National Association of Colleges and Employers

with a bachelor's degree vary by branch. Some examples appear on page 124.

A survey of workplaces in 160 metropolitan areas reported that beginning engineers had median annual earnings of roughly $34,400 in 1995, with the middle half earning between about $30,900 and $38,116 a year. Experienced mid-level engineers with no supervisory responsibilities had median annual earnings of about $59,100, with the middle half earning between about $54,000 and $65,000 a year. Median annual earnings for engineers at senior managerial levels were about $99,200.

The median annual salary for all engineers who worked full-time was about $49,200 in 1996. The average annual salary for engineers in the federal government was $61,950 in 1997. Those with a bachelor's degree had median annual earnings of $49,800; master's degree, $56,700; and PhD, $64,700.

Related Occupations

Other professionals who need similar skills are physical scientists, life scientists, computer scientists, mathematicians, engineering and science technicians, and architects.

Additional Information

American Institute of Aeronautics and Astronautics, Inc.
AIAA Student Programs
The Aerospace Center
370 L'Enfant Promenade SW
Washington, DC 20024-2518

American Institute of Chemical Engineers
345 E. 47th Street
New York, NY 10017-2395

American Chemical Society
Career Services
1155 16th Street NW
Washington, DC 20036

Institute of Industrial Engineers, Inc.
25 Technology Park/Atlanta
Norcross, GA 30092

American Society of Heating, Refrigerating, and Air-
    Conditioning Engineers, Inc.
1791 Tullie Circle NE
Atlanta, GA 30329

Society of Hispanic Professional Engineers
5400 E. Olympic Boulevard, Suite 210
Los Angeles, CA 90022
(213) 725-3970
http://www.shpe.net

The Minerals, Metals, and Materials Society
420 Commonwealth Drive
Warrendale, PA 15086-7514

The Society for Mining, Metallurgy, and Exploration, Inc.
PO Box 625002
Littleton, CO 80162-5002

American Nuclear Society
555 N. Kensington Avenue
LaGrange Park, IL 60525

Society of Petroleum Engineers
222 Palisades Creek Drive
Richardson, TX 75080

For information on electrical and electronic, civil, and mechanical
engineering, see their separate descriptions.

Electrical and Electronics Engineers

This is the largest engineering branch and the one projected to have more job openings in the next decade. As emerging markets attempt to compete in the global economy, they will need electrical and electronics engineers to develop equipment for their public utilities, telephone wiring, and other major systems.

The Job

Electrical and electronics engineers design, develop, test, and supervise the manufacture of electrical and electronic equipment. Electrical equipment includes electric motors, machinery controls, and lighting and wiring in buildings, automobiles, and aircraft. Electronic equipment includes radar, computer hardware, and communications and video equipment.

These professionals can specialize in one of several major areas such as communications, computer electronics, and electrical equipment manufacturing, or a subdivision of these areas such as aviation electronics. Electrical and electronics engineers design new products, write performance requirements, and develop maintenance schedules. They also test equipment, solve operating problems, and estimate the time and cost of engineering projects.

According to the Bureau of Labor Statistics, electrical and electronics engineers held about 367,000 jobs in 1996. Most work in engineering and business consulting firms, electrical and electronic equipment manufacturers, professional and scientific instruments, and government agencies. Most of the remaining jobs are in communications and utilities firms, industrial machinery manufacturers, and computer and data processing services firms.

(Note: for Education/Training, Career Mobility, Desired Characteristics, and Earnings see those sections in the general engineering description.)

Job Outlook

The Bureau of Labor Statistics projects that there will be 197,000 job openings for electrical and electronics engineers between 1996 and 2006, due to growth and job replacements. Employment growth will be driven by an increased demand for computers and communications equipment, as well as for electrical and electronic consumer goods. In addition, graduates who know the latest technologies will be needed to do research and development for the electronics manufacturing industry to remain competitive.

The Passion Factor: What do you like most about your occupation?

"I love it when the product does what I designed it to do," says Alfredo Martínez.

Born in Guatemala, he remembers being intrigued by electricity since he was a young child. "I used to take radios apart just to see what made them work."

Additional Information

Institute of Electrical and Electronics Engineers
1828 L Street NW, Suite 1202
Washington, DC 20036

Civil Engineers

"The job situation is competitive in this profession," said professor Chien Wu, head of the department civil and materials engineering at the University of Illinois at Chicago. "It is very helpful to know other languages."

The Job

Civil engineers design and supervise the construction of roads, airports, tunnels, bridges, water supply and sewage systems, and buildings. Major specialties within this branch are structural, water resources, environmental, construction, and transportation engineering. Many civil engineers hold supervisory or administrative positions, ranging from supervisor of a construction site to city engineer. Others may work in design, construction, research, and teaching.

According to the Bureau of Labor Statistics, civil engineers held about 196,000 jobs in 1996. They usually work near major industrial and commercial centers, often at construction sites. Some projects take them to remote areas or to foreign countries.

More than 40 percent of civil engineers work for federal, state, or local government agencies. Another 40 percent are employed in engineering consulting firms, primarily developing designs for new construction projects. The rest work in the construction industry, public utilities, transportation, and manufacturing industries.

(Note: for Education/Training, Career Mobility, Desired Characteristics, and Earnings see those sections in the general engineering description.)

Job Outlook

The Bureau of Labor Statistics projects that there will be 82,000 job openings for civil engineers between 1996 and 2006, due to growth and net replacements. Employment growth will be spurred by an expanding economy, where civil engineers will be needed to design and construct higher capacity transportation, water supply, and pollution control systems; large buildings and building complexes; and repair or replace existing roads, bridges, and other public structures.

The Passion Factor: What do you like most about your occupation?

"I tried mechanical and chemical engineering but I didn't like either of them," says Pedro Suárez. "When I discovered civil engineering I knew I had found my calling."

Born in Colombia, Suárez recalls that, in high school, he was good in math and physics. A friend's brother, who was a civil engineer, turned out to be his most important role model.

Additional Information

American Society of Civil Engineers
345 E. 47th Street
New York, NY 10017

Mechanical Engineers

Mechanical engineering is the broadest branch of this discipline, extending across a variety of interdependent specialties.

Some mechanical engineers work in production operations, maintenance, and technical sales. Others are administrators or managers.

The Job

Mechanical engineers design and develop power-producing and power-using machines. Power-producing machines include internal combustion engines, steam and gas turbines, and jet and rocket engines. Power-using machines include refrigeration and air-conditioning equipment, robots, and machine tools.

Specialties in this branch include applied mechanics, design engineering, heat transfer, pressure vessels and piping, and underwater technology. These engineers also design tools needed by other engineers.

According to the Bureau of Labor Statistics, mechanical engineers held about 228,000 jobs in 1996. Almost six out of ten jobs were in manufacturing—of these, most were in the machinery, transportation equipment, electrical equipment, instruments, and fabricated metal products industries. Business and engineering consulting services and federal government agencies provided most of the remaining jobs.

Job Outlook

The Bureau of Labor Statistics projects that there will be 81,000 job openings for mechanical engineers between 1996 and 2006, due to growth and net replacements. Driving employment growth will be the expected increased demand for machinery and machine tools.

(Note: for Education/Training, Career Mobility, Desired Characteristics, and Earnings see those sections in the general engineering description.)

Additional Information

The American Society of Mechanical Engineers
345 E. 47th Street
New York, NY 10017

Physical Sciences

In the occupational category of physical sciences, which includes agricultural and biological sciences, only the occupation of chemist fits our criteria.

Chemists

"Because of downsizing, it now takes longer for chemists to find entry-level positions," observed professor Jon Carnahan, director of the graduate chemistry department at Northern Illinois University. "Still, 98 percent of our graduates get jobs, especially in areas which are rich in chemical industries. And the bilingual students have a greater advantage. One of them was offered a job as a liaison with a manufacturing plant in Puerto Rico."

The Job

Chemists find practical uses for chemicals and invent new chemical compounds. Thanks to the work of these professionals, we have new and improved synthetic fibers, paints, adhesives, drugs, cosmetics, electronic components, lubricants, and many other products. Chemists also have found ways to save energy and reduce pollution by improving processing methods for such things as oil refining. Advances in medicine, agriculture, food processing, and other areas are often the result of research on the chemistry of living things.

Some chemists work in research and development. In basic research, they analyze the properties, composition, and structure of matter. In applied research and development, chemists devise new products and processes or improve existing ones.

Other chemists are employed in chemical manufacturing plants where they work in production and quality control. Some chemists are marketing or sales representatives who sell and provide technical information on chemical products.

Chemists often specialize in a particular field. **Analytical chemists** ascertain the structure, composition, and nature of substances and develop analytical techniques. For example, analysis allows chemists to identify which chemical pollutants are present in air, water, and soil and in what concentrations. **Organic chemists** study the chemistry of carbon compounds. They have developed many commercial products, such as drugs, plastics, and fertilizers. **Inorganic chemists** study compounds without carbon, such as electronic components. **Physical chemists** investigate how chemical reactions work. The work of **biochemists** combines biology and chemistry.

Most chemists work in manufacturing firms and primarily in the chemical manufacturing industry, which produces plastics and synthetic materials, drugs, soaps and cleaners, paints, industrial organic chemicals, and other miscellaneous chemical products. Some chemists work for state and local governments, mostly in health and agriculture, and for federal agencies, such as the Departments of Defense, Health and Human Services, and Agriculture. Others work for research and testing services. In addition, others teach chemistry in colleges and universities.

According to the Bureau of Labor Statistics, chemists held about 91,000 jobs in 1996. While they work in all parts of the country, they are mainly concentrated in large industrial areas.

Education/Training

Usually, a bachelor's degree in chemistry or a related discipline is the minimum education necessary to work as a chemist. However, the vast majority of research jobs require a PhD degree.

Most graduate students specialize in a chemistry field. However, specialization is not recommended at the undergraduate level. Undergraduates with broad training can be more flexible when they look for or change jobs. Most employers will provide new bachelor's degree chemists with additional training or education.

Beginning chemists with a bachelor's degree who are employed in government or industry usually work in technical sales or services, quality control, or assist senior chemists in research and development laboratories. Some may work in research positions, analyzing and testing products, but these may be technicians' positions, with limited promotion opportunity.

Career Mobility

In general, advancement to many administrative positions requires a PhD. Chemists who work in sales, marketing, or professional research positions often move into management eventually.

Some chemists who have bachelor's degrees move into other occupations in which their training is helpful. They can become technical writers or sales representatives in chemical marketing. Some enter health profession schools such as those that have medical, dental, or veterinary programs.

Some chemistry graduates become high school teachers, and those with a PhD may teach at the college or university level.

Desired Characteristics

Chemists should like science and mathematics, and enjoy working to build scientific apparatus and perform experiments. The ability to concentrate on detail, perseverance, and curiosity are essential characteristics. Knowledge of computer sciences is a great asset because most employers seek applicants who can apply computer skills to modeling and simulation tasks. Laboratory instruments are also computerized, and the ability to operate and understand equipment is crucial.

Having an understanding of other disciplines, such as business and marketing or economics, is suitable because research and development chemists are expected to work in interdisciplinary teams. Leadership ability, along with good oral and written communication skills, are a plus. Experience, either in academic laboratories or through internships or co-op programs in industry, is useful. Some employers of research chemists, particularly in the pharmaceutical industry, prefer to hire individuals with several years of postdoctoral experience.

Job Outlook

The Bureau of Labor Statistics projects that there will be 36,000 jobs for chemists through the year 2006, due to growth and net replacements. Analytical, environmental, and synthetic organic chemists should have the best job prospects. Employment growth will be driven by the increasing demand for goods such as new and better pharmaceuticals and personal care products, as well as more specialized chemicals designed to address specific problems or applications.

Competition among drug companies and an aging population are among the several factors that contribute to the need for innovative and improved drugs discovered through scientific research. Job opportunities are expected to be most plentiful in pharmaceutical and biotechnological firms.

While employment growth is expected to be slower in the remaining segments of the chemical industry, there will still be a need for chemists to develop and improve products, such as cosmetics and cleansers, as well as develop and improve the technologies and processes used to produce chemicals. Job growth will also be spurred by the need for chemists to monitor and measure air and water pollutants to ensure compliance with local, state, and federal environmental regulations.

Earnings

According to a survey by the American Chemical Society, the median annual salary of all their members with a bachelor's degree was $49,400 in 1997; with a master's degree, $56,200; and with a PhD, $71,000. Median salaries were highest for those working in private industry; those in academia earned the least. According to an ACS survey of recent graduates, first-time hires with a bachelor's degree earned a median starting salary of $25,000 in 1996; with a master's degree, $31,100; and with a PhD, $45,000. Among graduates holding bachelor's degrees, those who had completed internships or had other work experience while in school commanded the highest starting salaries.

In 1997, chemists in nonsupervisory, supervisory, and managerial positions in the federal government earned an average salary of $60,000.

The Passion Factor: What do you like most about your occupation?

"I like the fact that each day I have to do new things and I learn something," says Mariana Domínguez, a chemist with a bachelor's degree in analytical chemistry, and a PhD in electrical chemistry. "In trying to come up with answers I use all the concepts I learned as a student."

Born in Costa Rica, Domínguez chose this field because she admired her high school chemistry teacher. Now employed in a large research company, she develops lithium secondary batteries—those which are commonly used in calculators and watches.

Related Occupations

Other professionals whose occupation requires similar skills include chemical engineers, agricultural scientists, biological scientists, chemical technicians, physicists, and medical scientists.

Additional Information

American Chemical Society
Department of Career Services
1155 16th Street NW
Washington, DC 20036

Information on federal job opportunities is available from local offices of state employment services or offices of the U.S. Office of Personnel Management, located in major metropolitan areas.

Sales and Marketing Careers

There are many reasons why a career in sales is particularly good for Latinos. As we mentioned in earlier chapters, the median U.S. Latino household income has more than doubled since 1980, and our combined buying power is estimated to be over $273 billion. There is a ripe and growing market if you choose to specialize in the sale of consumer products and services. And, if you are bilingual, the future looks even better.

"Sales [are] about relationship-building," says Hyacinth Robertson, an insurance and financial services sales professional. "Any language you speak in addition to English—particularly in urban areas—doubles your assets."

Being bilingual and bicultural, as well as having a natural ability to build good relationships, are also assets in another sales arena. Professionals with such a background are in high demand and quite valuable to multinational companies. As these businesses move their goods and services into emerging markets—the frontiers that opened with globalization—they need people who can develop and maintain successful sales territories.

"The Anglo society has been more individualistic," observes Mariita Conley, of Conley, Arosemena & Associates, a Chicago-based firm that offers multicultural customer service and leadership training to large corporations. "Latinos are good at consensus building—we know how to do teamwork—and this approach always has worked much better overseas."

As we know, it now also works in the domestic U.S. market, where several sales occupations are expected to grow considerably in the next decade. Jobs for retail salespersons, marketing and sales supervisors, securities and financial sales workers, and general managers and top executives (many of whom rose through the sales ranks) will be plentiful. They all appear in one or both of the tables included in Chapter 4.

In fact, Conley suggests that those of you who are interested in foreign markets first explore the opportunities your current employer might be able to offer. "The best place to start is where you're at," she says with conviction. "If you know your company needs people to work in expanding markets, you can approach them and say: 'Here's why you should send *me* there.'"

An Informed Decision

Although the income range is wide, the upper-end sales careers can be quite lucrative. Depending on what he or she sells, a salesperson can earn anywhere between $16,000 and well over $100,000 per year. Compensation systems vary, but most sales workers are paid a commission or a combination of wages and commissions. Under a commission system, salespersons receive a percentage of the sales they make. Employers also use incentive programs such as awards, banquets, and profit-sharing plans to promote teamwork among the sales staff.

"I haven't made less than six figures since 1986," Hyacinth Robertson confesses.

Clearly, these markets present a vast array of opportunities. However, many Latinos do not take advantage of them. While the sales world has the lure of high earnings potential, ironically people often rule it out because of the uncertainty of its income. Most people need—psychologically and literally—to get a paycheck on a regular basis.

But Robertson says that you *can* become a salesperson without being evicted from your home. As one of the participants in a panel discussion organized by Women Employed, she proposes that the key is to plan for it.

The First Two Years

Generally, it takes a couple of years to build relationships and develop a sales territory—whether it is because you are just starting out or because you are switching products or territories. If you devise a strategy that will get you through the period of uncertainty, you are more than likely to reap the rewards.

The Women Employed panel, made up of several salespeople representing a variety of industries, recommends these steps to survive the first two years.

Start with a company that provides training and pays you a base salary while you are being trained. The best companies to work for tend to be the larger ones because they are willing to invest in you until you become more marketable.

Negotiate a fixed salary for the longest possible period of time. "Most companies have a plan to get you over the first two years when you will face ups and downs. They might even ask you to prepare a *personal* budget to see what you will need," explains Robertson.

Save money *before* you get into sales. "I planned for it," said Nancy O'Brien, an account executive in the brokerage industry. "I refinanced the house and paid off the car."

If you like an industry in which everyone works strictly on commission, find a part-time job to supplement your income.

Talk to your family and friends about the step you are about to take. You will need their moral (and sometimes financial) support until the commissions begin to come in.

What to Sell

If you have decided that sales is your calling, but you don't know what you would like to sell, the panelists had this to say:

Ask yourself: Who do I want to be talking to all day long?

"It is a very different experience to sell services to a corporate executive [such as training programs for his company] than to sell merchandise to the manager of a gym," Joan Smith, former program director at Women Employed, points out.

Find out what is the sales cycle for the product. If you are selling computers, for example, you might have to spend a great deal of time educating the customer about your product. The longer it takes to close the sale, the longer it will take for you to get your commission. "In high tech, the sky is the limit," observed Alice Prais, who sells business machines and computer software. "The decision-makers have to move fast."

Look for companies that sell quality products. It will make your job easier, not only in terms of the sale but also in terms of customer satisfaction.

If you have never sold a thing, network to find out which companies hire people without experience.

Who Succeeds

While some of the qualities you need to succeed in sales will vary according to your industry, the "raw materials" are the same no matter what you sell. Check the following list and see if you find a fit with your personality.

Successful salespeople:

Are goal-oriented.

Persevere; they think of obstacles as successes waiting to happen.

Think "outside the box."

Have high energy, are flexible, know how to negotiate (so they can hold deals together), and have patience.

Are able to communicate with a variety of people at different levels within an organization.

Know and enjoy the product they sell.

Are able to deal with rejection.

Have self-confidence and believe in the company they work for.

Have an employer who provides sales training and client support so they can service their accounts.

Follow up; they not only take care of their clients when they want them to buy a product, but also after the sale to make sure everyone is satisfied.

Stay current in their field by reading or taking courses to remain marketable.

This is how O'Brien sums up why she likes sales: "It's like having your own business but with the backing of the company."

Below are the specific possibilities the domestic market has to offer. The occupations are retail sales workers, supervisors and managers, insurance agents and brokers, sales service representatives, and travel agents.

Retail Sales

"Most of the major stores think of the sales ranks as a source for getting future executives," said a spokesperson for the National Retail Federation. "They look for people who are bright, aggressive, and willing to learn."

The Job

In retail, the primary job of a salesperson is to help customers find what they want and to interest them in buying the goods. Depending on the product, the salesperson may have to describe its features, show the customer how it works, and present alternate models and colors. The salesperson who sells "big-ticket items," such as refrigerators, televisions, copy machines or computers, needs to have more specialized knowledge of such products. He or she may have to answer customers' questions about the merchandise, explain its features, the different brands and models, and the meaning of manufacturers' specifications.

The majority of retail sales workers, particularly those who are employed in department and apparel stores, also make out sales checks; receive cash, check, and charge payments; bag or wrap purchases; and give change and receipts. Depending on the hours they work, they may have to open or close the cash register. Salespersons also may handle returns and exchanges of merchandise, wrap gifts, mark price tags, take inventory, and prepare displays.

According to the Bureau of Labor Statistics, retail salespersons held about 4,522,000 jobs in 1996. Most worked in stores, ranging from small specialty shops employing several workers to the giant department store with hundreds of salespersons. In addition, some were self-employed representatives of direct-sales companies and mail-order houses. The largest employers of retail sales workers, however, were department stores, clothing and accessories stores, motor vehicle dealers, and grocery stores.

Education/Training

Normally, there are no formal education requirements for a salesperson. However, those who are interested in a retail sales career do need a college degree with an emphasis on retailing or marketing. Most stores provide their new employees with an orientation session. Larger stores have more formal training programs that may last several days. Instruction varies with the type of products the store sells; the more complex the item, the more knowledge the new employee will need.

Career Mobility

As salespersons gain experience and seniority, they usually move to positions of greater responsibility and are given their choice of departments. This often means moving to areas with potentially higher earnings and commissions (normally the big-ticket items).

A faster route to promotions is often found in stores with several branches, where salespeople advance from the floor to store manager, then to area manager, and so on.

Desired Characteristics

Salespersons should enjoy working with people, and have tact and patience to deal with difficult customers. They must have a neat appearance, and the ability to communicate clearly and effectively.

Salespersons should be courteous and efficient because the retail industry is very competitive and, increasingly, employers are stressing the importance of providing excellent customer service. They also must be honest (salespersons may be held responsible for the contents of their register); and vigilant (they often must recognize possible security risks and know how to handle such situations).

Attitude is particularly important in this business. "If you want to be a manager, begin acting like one," urges Joseph Siegel of the National Retail Federation.

Job Outlook

According to the Bureau of Labor Statistics, there will be about 1,701,000 job openings for retail salespersons, due to growth and net replacements between 1996 and 2006. Growth in employment will be driven in great measure by replacement of the salespeople who move on. A projected increase in retail sales also will spur demand.

Earnings

The Bureau of Labor Statistics reports that the starting wage for many retail sales positions is the federal minimum wage, which was $5.15 an hour in 1997. In some areas where employers are having difficulty attracting and retaining workers, wages are higher than the established minimum. The following examples show 1996 median weekly earnings by class of sales worker:

Class of Sales Worker	Median Weekly Earnings
Motor vehicles and boats	$593
Radio, television, hi-fi, and appliances	423
Parts	409
Furniture and home furnishings	403
Apparel	265

Source: Bureau of Labor Statistics, U.S. Department of Labor

Compensation systems vary by type of establishment and merchandise sold. Sales workers receive either hourly wages, commissions, or a combination of wages and commissions. This system offers sales workers the opportunity to significantly increase their earnings, but they may find their earnings depend on their ability to sell their product and the ups and downs of the economy. Employers may use incentive programs such as awards, banquets, and profit-sharing plans to promote teamwork among the sales staff.

Benefits may be limited in smaller stores, but in large establishments benefits are usually comparable to those offered by other employers. In addition, nearly all sales workers are able to buy their store's merchandise at a discount, with the savings depending on the type of merchandise.

The Passion Factor: What do you like most about your occupation?

"When I help a customer choose the right outfit for her body type and skin complexion, I feel very creative," says Sylvia Moreno, a sales associate at a women's clothing store. "I know she'll look great when she wears it and will probably come back to this store, and to me, the next time she needs to buy clothes."

Moreno, who always wanted to be surrounded by "nice, fluffy fabrics," readily admits that the clothing discounts she gets are an added and welcome perk of her job.

Related Occupations

Other professionals whose occupation requires similar skills are manufacturers' and wholesale trade sales representatives, service sales representatives, securities and financial services sales representatives, counter and rental clerks, real estate sales agents, purchasers and buyers, insurance agents and brokers, and cashiers.

Additional Information

National Retail Federation
325 Seventh Street NW, Suite 1000
Washington, DC 20004-2802

Retail Sales Worker Supervisors and Managers

If you are interested in a retail sales career, this is your next step after gaining experience on the sales floor. You will broaden the ranks of Latino managers who are mentoring tomorrow's sales leaders.

The Job

Retail supervisors and managers oversee the work of sales associates, cashiers, customer service workers, stock and inventory clerks, and grocery clerks. Retail supervisors and managers also are responsible for interviewing, hiring, and training employees, as well as preparing work schedules and assigning workers to their specific duties.

The responsibilities of retail sales worker supervisors and managers vary depending on the size and type of establishment as well as the level of management. In general, in the larger retail store these workers are more specialized. For example, they can specialize in one department such as crystal or one aspect of merchandising such as sporting goods. Larger organizations tend to have many layers of management. Similar to other industries, supervisory-level retail managers usually report to their mid-level counterparts who, in turn, report to top-level managers. Small stores and stores that carry specialized merchandise typically have fewer levels of management.

Supervisory-level retail managers, often known as **department managers**, provide the day-to-day oversight of individual departments such as shoes, cosmetics, or housewares in large department stores; produce and meat in grocery stores; and service and sales in automotive dealerships. They usually work in large retail stores. They establish and implement policies, goals, objectives, and procedures for their specific departments; coordinate activities with other department heads; and strive for smooth operations within their departments. They supervise employees who price and ticket goods and place goods on display; review inventory and sales records, develop merchandising techniques, and coordinate sales promotions.

In smaller or independent retail stores, these professionals not only directly supervise sales associates, but are also responsible for the operation of the entire store. In these instances, they may also be called a **store manager**.

According to the Bureau of Labor Statistics, retail salespersons' supervisors and managers who work in retail trade held about 929,000 wage and salary jobs in 1996. In addition, there were thousands of self-employed retail sales managers, mainly store owners. Managers are found in every retail trade industry—grocery stores, department stores, clothing and shoe stores, automotive dealers, and furniture stores are among the largest industries.

Education/Training

The essential requirement for a management position in retail trade is knowledge of management principles and practices. Such knowledge usually is acquired through work experience. Many supervisors and managers begin their careers on the sales floor as sales clerks, cashiers, or customer service workers. In these positions they learn merchandising, customer service, and the basic policies and procedures of the store. And in many stores, this experience is required.

While educational backgrounds vary widely, retail supervisors and managers can benefit from such business courses as accounting, administration, marketing, management, and sales, as well as courses in psychology, sociology, and communication. They also must be computer literate as cash registers and inventory control systems become more computerized. Most supervisors and managers who have post-secondary education hold an associate's or a bachelor's degree in liberal arts, social science, business, or management.

Many national chains have formal training programs for management trainees, which include both classroom and in-store training. Training may last from one week to one year or more, as many retail organizations require their trainees to gain experience during all shopping seasons. Other retail organizations may not have formal training programs.

Franchises generally offer extensive training programs, covering all functions of the operation, including promotion, marketing, management, finance, purchasing, product preparation, human resource management, and compensation. College graduates usually enter management training programs directly.

Career Mobility

Individuals who display leadership skills, self-confidence, motivation, and decisiveness become candidates for promotion to assistant store manager or store manager. Increasingly, a postsecondary degree is needed for advancement because it is viewed by employers as a sign of motivation and maturity—qualities deemed important for promotion to more responsible positions. In many retail establishments, managers are promoted from within the company.

In small retail establishments, where the number of positions is limited, advancement to a higher management position may come slowly. Larger establishments have more extensive career ladder programs and offer managers the opportunity to transfer to another store in the chain or to the central office if an opening occurs. Promotion may occur more quickly in larger establishments, but relocation every several years may be necessary for advancement.

Positions within the central office to which sales supervisors and managers can move include marketing, advertising, and public relations managers, who coordinate marketing plans, monitor sales, and propose advertisements and promotions, and purchasers and buyers, who purchase goods and supplies for their organization or for resale.

Desired Characteristics

Retail managers must get along with all kinds of people. They need initiative, self-discipline, good judgment, and decisiveness. Patience and a mild temperament also come in handy when dealing with demanding customers. They also must be able to motivate, organize, and direct the work of subordinates, as well as communicate clearly and persuasively with customers and other managers.

Job Outlook

The Bureau of Labor Statistics projects that there will be 618,000 job openings for retail supervisors and managers through the year 2006 due to growth and net replacements. Among other factors, employment growth will be driven by an increase in number and size of grocery stores, department stores, automotive dealerships, and other retail establishments. As retailers try to accommodate consumers' desires for a greater selection of merchandise and one-stop shopping, the size of their establishments has been increasing. The specialization arising from creation of new departments within existing stores and the offering of additional product lines should spur the demand for store-level retail sales worker supervisors and managers.

Projected employment growth of retail managers will mirror, in part, the patterns of employment growth in industries in which they are concentrated. For example, faster than average growth is expected in miscellaneous shopping goods stores and in appliance, radio, television, and music stores. Average growth is expected in drugstores and proprietary stores, shoe stores, gasoline service stations, and motor vehicle dealers. On the other hand, slower than average growth is expected in department stores.

Unlike middle- and upper-level management positions, store-level retail supervisors and managers generally will not be affected by the restructuring and consolidating that is currently taking place at the corporate and headquarters level of many retail chain companies.

Earnings

Salaries of retail managers vary substantially, depending upon the level of responsibility; length of service; and type, size, and location of the firm. According to the Bureau of Labor Statistics, supervisors or managers of sales workers in the retail trade industry who usually worked full-time had median annual earnings of $24,400 in 1996. The middle 50 percent earned between $16,900 and $34,400. The top 10 percent earned more than $50,400, and the lowest 10 percent earned less than $12,900.

A survey sponsored by the National Association of Convenience Stores revealed that the average total compensation for assistant store managers in the U.S. and Canada ranged between $12,400 and $15,800 a year in 1996, depending on where the organization is located. Store managers received between $24,400 and $31,200 on average.

Compensation systems vary by type of establishment and merchandise sold. Many managers receive a commission, or a combination of salary and commission. Those managers who sell large amounts of merchandise often are rewarded with bonuses and awards and receive recognition throughout the store or chain.

Retail managers receive typical benefits and, in some cases, stock options. In addition, retail managers generally are able to buy their store's merchandise at a discount.

The Passion Factor: What do you like most about your occupation?

"I love the chance to deal one-on-one with my customers," says Juan Pérez, manager of the men's department at a large department store. "Each day at work is different, challenging, and fun because I deal with so many different people....I just couldn't be confined to an office."

Originally from Cuba, Pérez took college classes for one year. "But I'm not the studious type," he confesses. His first position at this store was as a stock associate. "It gave me an excellent perspective. In retail, you have to learn from the bottom up."

Related Occupations

Other professionals whose occupation requires similar skills are managers in wholesale trade, hotels, banks, hospitals, law firms, and a wide range of other industries.

Additional Information

National Retail Federation
325 Seventh Street NW, Suite 1000
Washington, DC 20004-2802

Food Marketing Institute
800 Connecticut Avenue NW
Washington, DC 20006-2701

National Automobile Dealers Association
8400 Westpark Drive
McLean, VA 22102-3591

National Association of Convenience Stores
1605 King Street
Alexandria, VA 22314

Service Station Dealers of America
9420 Annapolis Road, Suite 307
Lanham, MD 20706

Insurance Agents and Brokers

As Latino incomes rise, the insurance industry will reap many of
the benefits. For example, a large percentage of our families do
not have health insurance or are underinsured.

The Job

Insurance agents and brokers sell insurance policies to individuals and businesses to provide protection against loss. They help
their clients select the policy that provides the best insurance
protection for their lives and health, as well as for their automobiles, jewelry, personal valuables, furniture, household items, businesses, and other properties. In the event of a loss, agents and
brokers help policyholders settle insurance claims.

Specialists in group policies may help an employer provide
employees the opportunity to buy insurance through payroll de-
ductions. **Insurance agents** may work for one insurance company or as "independent agents" selling for several companies.
Insurance brokers do not sell for a particular company, but
place insurance policies for their clients with the company that offers the best rate and coverage.

Insurance agents sell one or more of several types of insurance: life, property and casualty, health, disability, and long-term
care. Life insurance agents specialize in selling policies that pay
beneficiaries when a policyholder dies. Property and casualty insurance agents and brokers sell policies that protect individuals
and businesses from financial loss as a result of automobile acci-

dents, fire or theft, tornadoes and storms, and other events that can damage property. For businesses, they can also cover injured workers' compensation, product liability claims, or medical malpractice payments. Many life, property, and casualty insurance agents also sell health insurance policies that cover some or all of the costs of hospital and medical care, or loss of income due to illness or injury.

An increasing number of insurance agents and brokers offer comprehensive financial planning services to their clients, such as retirement planning counseling. As a result, many insurance agents and brokers are also licensed to sell mutual funds, annuities, and other securities.

According to the Bureau of Labor Statistics, insurance agents and brokers held about 409,000 jobs in 1996. About three out of ten agents and brokers were self-employed. While most insurance agents specialize in life insurance, a growing number of "multi-line agents" offer life, property/casualty, health, and disability policies. Some insurance agents and brokers are employed in the headquarters of insurance companies, but the majority work out of local company offices or independent agencies.

Education/Training

Most companies and independent agencies prefer to hire college graduates—particularly those who have majored in business or economics—for jobs selling insurance. But most entrants to agent and broker jobs transfer from other occupations. As a result, these professionals tend to be older than the entrants of many other occupations.

Many colleges and universities offer courses in insurance, and some schools offer a bachelor's degree in insurance. College courses in finance, mathematics, accounting, economics, business law, government, and business administration enable insurance agents or brokers to understand how social, marketing, and economic conditions relate to the insurance industry. It is important for insurance agents and brokers to keep up to date with issues concerning clients. Changes in tax laws, government benefit programs, and other state and federal regulations can affect the insurance needs of clients and how agents conduct business. Basic familiarity with computers and popular software packages is very important. The use of computers to provide instantaneous information on a wide variety of financial products has greatly improved agents' and brokers' efficiency and enabled them to devote more time to clients.

Insurance agents and brokers must obtain a license in the states where they plan to sell insurance. Agents and brokers who plan to sell mutual funds and other securities must also obtain a separate securities license. New agents usually receive training in a classroom setting at pre-licensing schools conducted by state insurance agents associations or at the home offices of the insurance company. Often they attend company-sponsored classes to prepare for examinations. Others study on their own and accompany experienced agents when they call on prospective clients.

As the diversity of financial products sold by insurance agents and brokers increases, employers are placing greater emphasis on continuing professional education. In 1995, forty-three states had mandatory continuing education requirements focusing on insurance laws, consumer protection, and the technical details of various insurance policies.

Career Mobility

An insurance agent who shows sales ability and leadership may become a sales manager in a local office. A few advance to agency superintendent or executive positions. However, many who have built up a good clientele prefer to remain in sales work. Some, particularly in the property/casualty field, establish their own independent agencies or brokerage firms.

Desired Characteristics

Developing a satisfied clientele who will recommend an agent's services to other potential customers is a key to success in this field. Insurance agents and brokers should be enthusiastic, outgoing, self-confident, disciplined, hardworking, and able to communicate effectively. They should have the ability to inspire customer confidence. Because they usually work without supervision, agents and brokers must be able to plan their time well and have the initiative to locate new clients.

Job Outlook

The Bureau of Labor Statistics projects 95,000 job openings for insurance agents through the year 2006, due to growth and net replacements. Insurance sales are likely to increase because of the growing number of working women. Rising incomes as well as a concern for financial security should stimulate sales of mutual funds, variable annuities, and other financial products and services. Growing demand for long-term health care and pension benefits for retirees—an increasing proportion of the population—should spur insurance sales.

Sales of property and casualty insurance should rise as more people seek coverage not only for their homes, cars, and valuables, but also for expensive, advanced technology products such as home computers. As new businesses emerge and existing firms expand coverage, sales of commercial insurance should increase. In addition, complex types of commercial coverage such as product liability, workers' compensation, employee benefits, and pollution liability insurance are increasingly in demand.

Employment of agents and brokers will not keep pace with the rising level of insurance sales. Customer service representatives are increasingly assuming some sales functions, such as expanding accounts, and, occasionally, generating new accounts.

Opportunities should be best for ambitious people who enjoy sales work and who develop expertise in a wide range of insurance and financial services.

Earnings

According to the Bureau of Labor Statistics, the median annual earnings of salaried insurance sales workers was $31,500 in 1996. The middle 50 percent earned between $21,100 and $49,000 a year. The lowest 10 percent earned $15,000 or less, while the top 10 percent earned over $76,900.

Many independent agents are paid by commission only, whereas sales workers who are employees of an agency may be paid in one of three ways: salary, salary plus commission, or salary plus bonus. Commissions, however, are the most common form of compensation, especially for experienced agents. The amount of the commission depends on the type and amount of insurance sold, and whether the transaction is a new policy or a renewal. Bonuses are usually awarded when agents meet their sales goals or when an agency's profit goals are met. Some agents involved with financial planning receive an hourly fee for their services rather than a commission.

Company-paid benefits to sales agents generally include continuing education, paid licensing training, group insurance plans, and office space and clerical support services. Some may pay for automobile and transportation expenses, attendance at conventions and meetings, promotion and marketing expenses, and retirement plans. Independent agents working for insurance agencies receive fewer benefits, but their commissions may be higher to help them pay for promotion and marketing expenses. They are typically responsible for their own travel and automobile expenses, life insurance, and retirement plans. In addition, all agents are legally responsible for any mistakes that they make, and independent agents must purchase their own insurance to cover damages from their errors and omissions.

The Passion Factor: What do you like most about your occupation?

"What I like most about my job is the constant interaction with clients," says Roberto Flores, an agent working for a large insurance concern.

Born in New Mexico, Flores chose this line of work because there was a recession when he graduated with a master's degree in business. "Insurance is one of the industries that remain relatively stable in recessionary times," he explains. "By the time the economy improved I was so satisfied with my work, I had no desire to make a change."

Related Occupations

Other professionals whose occupation requires similar skills are real estate agents and brokers, securities and financial services sales representatives, financial advisors, estate planning specialists, and manufacturers' sales workers.

Additional Information

> National Association of Life Underwriters
> 1922 F Street NW
> Washington, DC 20006

> Independent Insurance Agents of America
> 127 S. Peyton Street
> Alexandria, VA 22314

> National Association of Professional Insurance Agents
> 400 N. Washington Street
> Alexandria, VA 22314

> Society of Certified Insurance Counselors
> 3630 N. Hills Drive
> Austin, TX 78731

Services Sales Representatives

Outside sales representatives who are responsible for a large territory may spend a great deal of time traveling, sometimes for weeks at a time. On the other hand, representatives with smaller territories may seldom, or never, travel overnight. Consider these factors in light of your family values before selecting the type of service you want to sell—and the size of the sales territory.

The Job

Services sales representatives sell services for a vast array of industries. For example, those who sell data-processing services market complex services such as inventory control or payroll processing. Hotel sales representatives solicit convention and conference business from government, business, and social groups. Those in the telephone services industry visit commercial customers to analyze their communications needs and recommend services, such as installation of additional equipment.

Services sales representatives act as industry experts, consultants, and problem solvers when selling their firm's services. In some cases, they actually create demand for their firm's services.

There are several categories of services sales jobs. **Outside sales representatives** call on clients and prospects at their homes or offices. **Inside sales representatives** work on their employer's premises, assisting individuals interested in the company's services. **Telemarketing sales representatives** sell over the telephone. Some sales representatives deal exclusively with one or a few major clients.

The jobs of all services sales representatives have much in common. All sales representatives must fully understand and be able to discuss the services their company offers. Many develop lists of prospective clients through telephone and business directories, asking business associates and customers for leads, and calling on new businesses as they cover their assigned territory.

All services sales representatives must show how the services offered meet the client's needs. Often, this involves demonstrations of the company's services. They also answer questions about the nature and cost of those services and try to overcome objections to persuade potential customers to purchase the services. After closing a sale, services sales representatives generally follow up to see that the purchase meets the customer's needs, and to determine if additional services can be sold. Good customer service is becoming increasingly important and can give a company a competitive advantage.

Services sales work varies with the kind of service sold. Selling highly technical services, such as communications systems or computer consulting services, involves complex and lengthy sales negotiations. In addition, sales of such complex services may require extensive post-sale support. In these situations, sales representatives may operate as part of a team of sales representatives and experts from other departments.

Usually, a sales representative handles a specific territory. A representative for a company offering services widely used by the general public, such as lawn care, generally has numerous clients in a relatively small territory. On the other hand, a sales representative for a more specialized organization, such as a standardized testing service, may need to service several states to acquire an adequate customer base.

According to the Bureau of Labor Statistics, services sales representatives held over 694,000 wage and salary jobs in 1996. More than half were in firms providing business services, including computer and data processing; personnel supply; advertising; mailing, reproduction, and stenographic services; and equipment rental and leasing. Other sales representatives worked for firms offering a wide range of other services, including those selected below.

Services Sales Employment by Industry

	Percent
Miscellaneous business services	26
Engineering and management services	11
Computer and data processing	10
Personnel supply service	10
Advertising	7
Amusement and recreation services	5
Personal services	5
Automotive repair services	4
Mailing, reproduction, and stenographic services	3
Membership organizations	3
Miscellaneous equipment rental and leasing	3
Health services	2
Hotels and other lodging places	2
Motion pictures	2
Social services	2
All other services	5

Source: *Occupational Outlook Handbook*, Bureau of Labor Statistics, U.S. Department of Labor

Education/Training

Depending on the industry a company represents, some employers may require services sales representatives to have a college degree. For example, employers who market advertising services are likely to seek individuals with a college degree in advertising, marketing or business administration. Companies marketing educational services probably prefer individuals with a degree in education, marketing, or a related field. Many hotels look for graduates from college hotel or tourism administration programs. Companies selling computer, communications, engineering, and other highly technical services generally require a bachelor's degree appropriate to their field. Certification and licensing is also becoming more common for technical sales representatives.

Employers who sell nontechnical services may hire sales representatives with only a high school diploma if they have a proven sales record. But applicants improve their chances of being hired into these positions if they have taken some college courses.

Many firms conduct intensive training programs for their sales representatives, including the uses of the service, effective prospecting methods, creating customer demand, closing a sale, communications technology, and the use of technical support personnel. Sales representatives may also attend seminars on a wide range of subjects given by outside or in-house training institutions.

Career Mobility

Sales representatives with good sales records and leadership ability may advance to supervisory and managerial positions. Frequent contact with business people in other firms provides sales workers with leads about job openings, enhancing advancement opportunities.

Desired Characteristics

Sales representatives should be persuasive and have a pleasant, outgoing, and enthusiastic disposition. They must be highly motivated, energetic, well organized, and efficient. Self-confidence, reliability, and the ability to communicate effectively both orally and in writing are essential. Sales representatives should be self-starters who have the ability to work under pressure to meet sales goals. They must also have a thorough knowledge of the service they are selling, and be able to anticipate and respond to their clients' questions and objections in a professional manner.

Job Outlook

According to the Bureau of Labor Statistics, employment of services sales representatives as a group is expected to grow much faster than the average for all occupations through the year 2006. This will be spurred by growth of the services industries employing them. However, the projected growth of particular services industries varies. For example, the continued growth in factory and office automation should lead to much faster-than-average employment growth for computer and data processing services sales representatives. Growth will be tempered in some industries by the expanded use of various technologies, such as voice and electronic mail, cellular telephones, and laptop computers, that increase sales representatives' productivity.

Openings also will occur because of the need to replace sales workers who transfer to other occupations or leave the labor force. Turnover is generally higher among representatives who sell nontechnical services, because they have invested less time and effort in specialized training. As a result of this turnover, job opportunities should be good, especially for those with a college degree or a proven sales record.

With improved technology, companies are finding it harder to justify the expense of travel, on-site presentations, waiting, and the preparation that supports those activities. Therefore, many companies are putting more emphasis on in-house sales by phone and other methods, and less emphasis on the use of outside sales staff. In addition, temporary or contract sales people are used more frequently for outside sales.

Earnings

According to the Bureau of Labor Statistics, the median annual income for full-time advertising sales representatives was $26,000 in 1996, while representatives selling other business services earned $30,264. Earnings of representatives who sold technical services were generally higher than earnings of those who sold nontechnical services.

Earnings of experienced sales representatives depend on performance. Successful sales representatives who establish a strong customer base can earn more than managers in their firm.

According to Dartnell Corporation's 1996 Sales Compensation Survey, entry-level sales representatives averaged $36,000 in total cash compensation, intermediate-level sales representatives earned $46,000, and senior sales representatives received $63,000.

As is the case with other sales professions, sales representatives are paid in a combination of salary and commissions. Some services sales representatives receive a base salary, plus incentive pay that can add 25 to 75 percent to the sales representative's base salary. In addition to the same benefits package received by other employees of the firm, outside sales representatives have expense accounts to cover meals and travel, and some drive a company car. Many employers offer bonuses, including vacation trips and prizes, for sales that exceed company quotas.

The Passion Factor: What do you like most about your occupation?

"I pride myself in selling an intricate service within a reasonable amount of time," says Ricardo Morales, who owns a data processing services company. "But what I like the most is seeing how well the systems work after the installation. The smile of a satisfied client is invaluable to me."

Originally from Mexico, Morales did not speak English when he came to the United States. Yet he chose a field in which communication is key to its success. "That's what motivated me to learn the English language. I started selling things when I was very young."

Related Occupations

Workers in other occupations requiring similar skills include real estate agents, insurance agents, securities and financial services sales representatives, retail sales workers, manufacturers' and wholesale sales representatives, and travel agents.

Additional Information

Sales and Marketing Executives International
6600 Hidden Lake Trail
Brecksville, OH 44141

Travel Agents

Being bilingual and bicultural is a definite plus in the tourism industry. Firsthand knowledge of a place is easier to sell to clients. And, when visiting a Spanish-speaking place, it opens many more doors.

The Job

Travel agents assess the needs of their clients and make the best possible travel arrangements for them. Depending on the needs of the client, travel agents may give advice on destinations, make arrangements for transportation, hotel accommodations, car rentals, tours, and recreation, or plan the right vacation package or business/pleasure trip combination. They may also advise on weather conditions, restaurants, and tourist attractions and recreation. For international travel, agents also provide information on customs regulations, required papers (passports, visas, and certificates of vaccination), and currency exchange rates.

Travel agents consult a variety of published and computer-based sources for information on departure and arrival times, fares, and hotel ratings and accommodations. They may visit hotels, resorts, and restaurants to judge, firsthand, comfort, cleanliness, and quality of food and service so they can base recommendations on their own travel experiences or those of colleagues or clients. Depending on the size of the travel agency, an agent may specialize by type of travel, such as leisure or business, or destination, such as Europe, Africa, or Latin America.

According to the Bureau of Labor Statistics, travel agents held about 142,000 jobs in 1996. More than nine out of ten salaried agents worked for travel agencies; some worked for membership organizations. About one out of ten agents were self-employed.

Education/Training

The minimum requirement is a high school diploma or equivalent. But formal or specialized training is becoming increasingly important because technology and computerization are having a profound effect on the work of travel agents. Many vocational schools offer six- to twelve-week full-time travel agent programs, as well as evening and Saturday programs. Travel courses are also offered in public adult education programs and in community and four-year colleges. A few colleges offer bachelor's or master's degrees in travel and tourism.

The American Society of Travel Agents (ASTA) offers a correspondence course that provides a basic understanding of the travel industry. Travel agencies also provide on-the-job training for their employees, a significant part of which consists of computer instruction. Computer skills are required by employers to operate airline and centralized reservation systems.

Experienced travel agents can take advanced self or group study courses from the Institute of Certified Travel Agents (ICTA) that lead to the designation of Certified Travel Counselor (CTC). The ICTA also offers sales skills development programs and destination specialist programs, which provide a detailed knowledge of the geographic areas of North America, Western Europe, the Caribbean, and the Pacific Rim.

There are no federal licensing requirements for travel agents. However, nine states require some form of registration or certification of retail sellers of travel services: California, Florida, Hawaii, Illinois, Iowa, Ohio, Oregon, Rhode Island, and Washington. More information may be obtained by contacting the Office of the Attorney General or Department of Commerce for each state.

Career Mobility

Some employees start as reservation clerks or receptionists in travel agencies. With experience and some formal training, they can take on greater responsibilities and eventually assume travel agent duties. In agencies with many offices, travel agents may advance to office manager or to other managerial positions.

Those who start their own agencies generally have experience in an established agency. They must generally gain formal supplier or corporation approval before they can receive commissions. Suppliers or corporations are organizations of airlines, ship lines, or rail lines.

Desired Characteristics

Although few college courses relate directly to the travel industry, a college education is sometimes desired by employers to establish a background in areas such as computer science, geography, communication, foreign languages, and world history. Courses in accounting and business management also are important, especially for those who expect to manage or start their own travel agencies. Other desirable qualifications include good word processing and letter writing skills, and an ability to work with computers.

Travel experience is an asset since personal knowledge about a city or foreign country often helps to influence clients' travel plans. Selling skills, patience, and the ability to gain the confidence of clients also are useful qualities.

Job Outlook

The Bureau of Labor Statistics projects that there will be 66,000 job openings for travel agents through the year 2006, due to growth and net replacements. Employment growth will be driven by the expected increase in travel spending—business as well as leisure. Business expansion and rising household incomes with smaller families will generate more trips which will be taken more frequently than in the past.

Some developments, however, may reduce opportunities for travel agents in the future. On-line computer systems now allow people to make their own travel arrangements. Suppliers of travel services are increasingly able to make their services available through less conventional means, such as electronic ticketing machines and remote ticket printers. Also, airline companies have put a cap on the amount of commissions they will pay to travel agencies. The full impact of these practices on travel agents, though, has yet to be determined. The travel industry generally is sensitive to economic downturns and political crises, when travel plans are likely to be deferred. Therefore, the number of job opportunities fluctuates.

Earnings

Experience, sales ability, and the size and location of the agency determine the salary of a travel agent. According to a Louis Harris survey, conducted for *Travel Weekly*, 1996 median annual earnings of travel agents on straight salary with less than one year experience were $16,400; from one to three years, $20,400; from three to five years, $22,300; from five to ten years, $26,300; and more than ten years, $32,600. Salaried agents usually have standard benefits, such as medical insurance coverage and paid vacations, that self-employed agents must provide for themselves. Among agencies, those focusing on corporate sales pay higher salaries and provide more extensive benefits, on average, than those who focus on leisure sales.

Earnings of travel agents who own their agencies depend mainly on commissions from airlines and other carriers, cruise lines, tour operators, and lodging places. Commissions for domestic travel arrangements, cruises, hotels, sightseeing tours, and car rentals are about 7 to 10 percent of the total sale; and for international travel, about 10 percent. They may also charge clients a service fee for the time and expense involved in planning a trip.

When they travel for personal reasons, agents usually get reduced rates for transportation and accommodations.

The Passion Factor: What do you like most about your occupation?

"I am doing what I always wanted to do," says Amalia Cordero, a travel agent who manages the tourism department in a mid-size agency. "Compared to other professions, this one is not particularly lucrative. But it has many other benefits. For example, when you travel you have the opportunity to see new places, meet people and grow as a person."

Related Occupations

Other professionals whose occupation requires similar skills are tour guides, meeting planners, airline reservation agents, rental car agents, and travel counselors.

Additional Information

American Society of Travel Agents
Education Department
1101 King Street
Alexandria, VA 22314

For information on certification qualifications, contact:

The Institute of Certified Travel Agents
148 Linden Street
PO Box 812059
Wellesley, MA 02181-0012

Education, Social Services, and Government Careers

For many Latinos, especially those who grew up in families that were always active in their communities, working in the public service arena is probably a natural progression in their lives. Having been close to the pulse of their neighborhoods, churches, and organizations, they became keenly aware of the particular needs and issues affecting their people.

Like health care, education and social services are most effective when delivered in the primary language of the recipient. For example, children who only speak Spanish cannot relate to their classmates or teachers and remain isolated in school. The language barrier also makes it difficult to identify those who might have special educational needs. Recent immigrant families also need help to navigate a new society with different social codes and languages.

Teachers and social workers are the professionals who attend to these community needs. At a different level, urban and regional planners who know and understand the community can have a significant impact on the revamping of old neighborhoods and the flow of public services such as transportation and sewer systems into those areas.

The Bureau of Labor Statistics projects that the number of jobs in education, special education, social work, and urban planning will increase faster or much faster than the average for all occupations through the year 2006. However, jobs in public service are particularly attractive to many people so the competition is intense. Speaking Spanish, particularly in urban areas, will place you at the very top of the applicants' list.

This chapter will describe the public service occupations mentioned above, along with their expected opportunities.

Education

The need for certified bilingual teachers is great, particularly in urban areas, where many school systems have sought teachers in Puerto Rico. With enrollments of minorities increasing, and a shortage of minority teachers, efforts to recruit minority teachers will intensify. Some states offer scholarships to those who commit to teaching in schools with a population of at least 30 percent minorities. Others offer scholarships to those willing to study and teach bilingual special education.

In addition to bilingual teachers and special education teachers, many schools are in need of other support personnel such as bilingual school psychologists and counselors.

School Teachers — Kindergarten, Elementary, and Secondary

Many of us have molded our ideas and made important life decisions because of the nurturing guidance of a favorite teacher. Whether or not bilingual education survives in this country's school systems beyond the '90s, teaching will give you the opportunity to help young Latinos stay in school and make the best possible choices for them.

The Job

Kindergarten and elementary school teachers generally teach five-to thirteen-year-olds. Their role in the development of children is pivotal, since children shape their views of themselves and the world during their early years. Those learning experiences also affect the children's later success or failure in school, work, and their personal lives. Kindergarten and elementary school teachers introduce children to numbers, language, science, and social studies. They use games, music, artwork, films, slides, computers, and other teaching tools to teach basic skills.

The majority of elementary school teachers have one class of children to whom they teach several subjects. In some schools, two or more teachers work as a team and are jointly responsible for a group of students in at least one subject. In other schools, a specialized teacher may teach music, art, reading, science, arithmetic, or physical education to a number of classes. A small but growing number of teachers instruct multilevel classrooms—those with students at several different learning levels.

Secondary school teachers generally teach fourteen- to seventeen-year olds. They help students to further explore the subjects introduced in elementary school and expose them to more information about the world and themselves. Secondary school teachers specialize in a specific subject, such as English, Spanish, mathematics, history, or biology. They teach a variety of related courses, such as American history, contemporary American problems, and world geography.

Today's teachers function as facilitators who use interactive approaches instead of lectures and rote memorization. For example, rather than merely telling students about a scientific event, teachers may ask students to perform a laboratory experiment and discuss how the results apply to the real world.

A major force behind the changes in education is the need to prepare students for the future workforce. That is why classes are becoming less structured, and students are working in groups to discuss and solve problems together. In the process, they learn to adapt to new technology, and think through problems logically.

Teachers may use films, slides, overhead projectors, and the latest technology in teaching, such as computers, telecommunication systems, and video discs. Telecommunication technology allows American students to communicate with students in other countries and share personal experiences or research projects of interest to both groups. Computers are used in many classroom activities, from helping students solve math problems to learning English as a second language. Increasingly, students are using the Internet for research and information gathering. Teachers must continually update their skills to use the latest technology in the classroom.

Because teachers work with students from increasingly diverse ethnic, racial, and religious backgrounds, they must learn about and establish rapport with a diverse student population. Their duties are wide-ranging and usually include assigning lessons, giving tests, listening to oral presentations, and maintaining classroom discipline. They also observe and evaluate a student's performance and potential, and increasingly use new assessment methods, such as examining a portfolio of a student's artwork or writing, to measure student achievement.

In addition to classroom activities, teachers plan and evaluate lessons, sometimes in collaboration with teachers of related subjects. They also prepare tests, grade papers, prepare report cards, oversee study halls and homerooms, supervise extracurricular activities, and meet with parents and school staff to discuss a student's academic progress or personal problems. They identify physical or mental problems and refer students to the proper agency for treatment. Secondary school teachers assist students in choosing courses, colleges, and careers. Teachers also participate in education conferences and workshops.

According to the Bureau of Labor Statistics, there are nearly 1.6 million kindergarten and elementary school teachers, and over 1.3 million secondary school teachers. Employment is distributed geographically, much the same as the population.

Education/Training

All fifty states and the District of Columbia require public school teachers to be licensed. Teachers may be licensed to teach the early childhood grades (usually nursery school through grade three); the elementary grades (grades one through six or eight); or a special subject, such as reading or music. Requirements for regular licenses vary by state. However, all states require a bachelor's degree and completion of an approved teacher training program with a prescribed number of subject and education credits and supervised practice teaching. Many states require teachers to obtain a master's degree in education, which involves at least one year of additional course work beyond the bachelor's degree with a specialization in a particular subject.

The National Council for Accreditation of Teacher Education currently accredits over 500 teacher education programs across the United States. Increasingly, more of them are offering a concentration in bilingual and/or multicultural education.

Many states offer alternative teacher licensure programs for people who have bachelor's degrees in the subject they will teach, but lack the necessary education courses required for a regular license. Alternative licensure programs were originally designed to ease teacher shortages in certain subjects, such as mathematics and science. The programs have expanded to attract other people into teaching, including recent college graduates and mid-career changers. They also exist, particularly in urban areas, to ease the shortage of bilingual teachers.

In some programs, individuals begin teaching quickly under provisional licensure. After working under the close supervision of experienced educators for one or two years while taking education courses outside school hours, they receive regular licensure if they have progressed satisfactorily. Under other programs, college graduates who do not meet licensure requirements take only those courses that they lack, and then become licensed. States may issue emergency licenses to individuals who do not meet requirements for a regular license when schools cannot attract enough qualified teachers to fill positions. Teachers who need licensure may enter programs that grant a master's degree in education, as well as licensure.

Almost all states require applicants for teacher licensure to be tested for competency in basic skills such as reading and writing, teaching skills, or subject matter proficiency. Most states require continuing education for renewal of the teacher's license; some require a master's degree. Many states have reciprocity agreements that make it easier for teachers licensed in one state to become licensed in another.

Recently, the National Board for Professional Teaching Standards began offering voluntary national certification for teachers. A teacher who is nationally certified may find it easier to obtain employment in another state.

Career Mobility

With additional preparation and certification or licensure, teachers may move into positions as reading specialists, curriculum specialists, or guidance counselors. Teachers may become administrators or supervisors, although the number of these positions is limited. In some systems, highly qualified, experienced teachers can become senior or mentor teachers, with higher pay and additional responsibilities. They guide and assist less experienced teachers while keeping most of their teaching responsibilities.

Desired Characteristics

Teachers must be knowledgeable in their subject. In addition, it is essential for teachers to have the ability to communicate, inspire trust and confidence, and motivate students, as well as understand their educational and emotional needs. They also should be organized, dependable, patient, and creative. Teachers must also be able to work cooperatively and communicate effectively with other teaching staff, support staff, and parents and other members of the community.

Job Outlook

The Bureau of Labor Statistics projects that there will be jobs for 190,000 preschool and kindergarten teachers, 438,000 elementary school teachers and 731,000 secondary school teachers through the year 2006. Employment growth will be driven, in part, by the large number of teachers now in their forties and fifties who will reach retirement age by the end of the decade.

Assuming relatively little change in average class size, employment growth of teachers depends on population growth rates and corresponding student enrollments. Enrollment of fourteen-to seventeen-year-olds is expected to grow through the year 2006, spurring demand for secondary school teachers. Enrollment of five- to thirteen-year olds also is projected to increase, but at a slower rate, resulting in divergent growth rates for individual teaching occupations.

The job market for teachers varies widely among states and school districts. Some central cities and rural areas have difficulty attracting enough teachers, so job prospects should continue to be better in these areas than in suburban districts. Teachers in some subjects, such as mathematics, chemistry, physics, bilingual education, and computer science are in short supply.

Earnings

According to the National Education Association, the estimated average salary of all public elementary and secondary school teachers in the 1995–96 school year was $37,900. Public secondary school teachers averaged about $38,600 a year, while public elementary school teachers averaged $37,300. Private school teachers generally earn less than public school teachers.

In 1996, more than half of all public school teachers belonged to unions—mainly the American Federation of Teachers and the National Education Association—that bargain with school systems over wages, hours, and the terms and conditions of employment.

In some schools, teachers receive extra pay for coaching sports and working with students in extracurricular activities. Some teachers earn extra income during the summer working in the school system or in other jobs.

The Passion Factor: What do you like most about your occupation?

"What I like most about my job is my students' enthusiasm for learning," says Sara Rodríguez, a high school mathematics teacher at an inner city school. "But I also like to see that, when I teach them something, they know how to apply it to real life."

Originally from Mexico, Rodríguez attended high school in Chicago and knew she wanted to teach since she was a little girl.

"I always enjoyed helping people understand things," she recalls. Inspired by her own high school math teacher, she now teaches algebra, geometry, and trigonometry.

Related Occupations

Other professionals whose occupation requires similar skills are college and university faculty, counselors, education administrators, employment interviewers, librarians, preschool teachers, public relations specialists, sales representatives, social workers, and trainers and employee development specialists.

Additional Information

Information on licensure or certification requirements and approved teacher training institutions is available from local school systems and state departments of education.

> American Federation of Teachers
> 555 New Jersey Avenue NW
> Washington, DC 20001

> National Education Association
> 1201 16th Street NW
> Washington, DC 20036

> National Council for Accreditation of Teacher Education
> 2010 Massachusetts Avenue NW
> 5th Floor
> Washington, DC 20036

> National Board for Professional Teaching Standards
> 300 River Place
> Detroit, MI 48207

School Teachers—Special Education

"This job takes a commitment that goes beyond just teaching," says professor Angela Miller of DePaul University. "A special education teacher has to work with students who have to struggle to be integrated into society. That is why it is so important to have Latino teachers as role models for them."

The Job

Special education teachers work with students who have a variety of disabilities. These include specific learning disabilities, mental retardation, speech or language impairment, serious emotional disturbance, visual and hearing impairment, orthopedic impairment, autism, traumatic brain injury, and other health impairments. Students are classified under one of the categories, and special education teachers are prepared to work with specific groups. They also work with students who have other special instructional needs, including those who are gifted and talented.

Although special education teachers can work with students ranging from toddlers to those in their early twenties, most are found at the elementary, middle, and secondary school level.

Special education teachers design and modify instruction to meet a student's special needs. Depending on the disability, teaching methods can include individualized instruction, problem-solving assignments, and group or individual work.

Special education teachers are legally required to participate in the development of an Individualized Education Program (IEP) for each special education student. The IEP sets personalized goals for each student and is tailored to a student's individual learning style and ability. This program includes a transition plan which outlines specific steps and procedures to prepare special education students for a job or for post-secondary study. Teachers review the IEP with the student's parents, school administrators, and often the student's general education teacher. Teachers work closely with parents to inform them of their child's progress and suggest techniques to promote learning at home.

Special education teachers are involved in their students' behavioral and academic development. They help them to develop emotionally, be comfortable in social situations, and be aware of socially acceptable behavior. Preparing special education students for daily life after graduation is an important aspect of the job. Teachers may help students with routine skills, such as balancing a checkbook, or provide them with career counseling.

As schools become more inclusive, special education teachers and general education teachers are working together in general education classrooms. Special education teachers help general educators adapt curriculum materials and teaching techniques to meet the needs of students with disabilities.

Some special education teachers have their own classrooms and teach classes made up entirely of special education students. Others work as special education resource teachers and offer individualized help to students in general education classrooms. Some teach along with general education teachers in classes composed of both general and special education students. Others work in a resource room, where students work several hours a day, separate from their general education classroom. A significantly smaller proportion of special education teachers work in residential facilities or tutor students in homebound or hospital environments.

Special education teachers must communicate frequently with social workers, school psychologists, occupational and physical therapists, parents, school administrators, and other teachers.

According to the Bureau of Labor Statistics, special education teachers held about 407,000 jobs in 1996. The vast majority worked in public schools. The rest were employed in separate educational facilities (public or private residential facilities) or in homebound or hospital environments. Employment is distributed geographically, much the same as the population.

Education/Training

All fifty states and the District of Columbia require special education teachers to be licensed. Special education licensure varies by state. In many states, special education teachers receive a general education credential to teach kindergarten through grade twelve. These teachers train in a specialty, such as teaching children with learning disabilities or behavioral disorders. Some states offer general special education licensure, others license several different specialties within special education, while others require teachers to first obtain general education licensure and then additional licensure in special education.

All states require a bachelor's degree and completion of an approved teacher preparation program with a prescribed number of subject and education credits and supervised practice teaching. Many states require special education teachers to obtain a master's degree in special education, involving at least one year of additional course work, including a specialization, beyond the bachelor's degree.

About 700 colleges and universities across the United States offer programs in special education, including undergraduate, master's, and doctoral programs. Special education teachers usually undergo longer periods of training than general education teachers. Most bachelor's degree programs are four-year programs that include general and specialized courses in special education. However, an increasing number of institutions require a fifth year or other post-baccalaureate preparation. In addition, some experimental bilingual programs are being created now. Some programs require a specialization, such as teaching students with specific learning disabilities. Others offer generalized special education degrees, or study in several specialized areas. The last year of the program is usually spent student teaching in a classroom supervised by a certified teacher.

Alternative and emergency licensure is available in many states due to the need to fill special education teaching positions. In some programs, individuals begin teaching quickly under provisional licensure, while taking education courses. Some bilingual special education aides have taken advantage of these programs to be able to teach. Emergency licensure is enacted when states are having difficulty finding licensed special education teachers to fill positions.

Career Mobility

Special education teachers can advance to become supervisors or administrators. They may also earn advanced degrees and become instructors in colleges that prepare other special education teachers.

Desired Characteristics

Special education teachers must be able to motivate students, understand their special needs, and be accepting of differences in others. They must be creative and able to apply different types of teaching methods to reach students who are having difficulties. Communication and cooperation are also essential traits since special education teachers spend a great deal of time interacting with others, including students, parents, and school faculty and administrators.

Job Outlook

The Bureau of Labor Statistics projects that there will be 299,000 openings for special education teachers through the year 2006, due to growth and net replacements. Employment growth will be spurred by an expected increase in the number of special education students needing services, legislation emphasizing training and employment for individuals with disabilities, growing public interest in individuals with special needs, and educational reform.

Many job openings also arise when special education teachers switch to general education or change careers altogether. Job openings stemming from rapid employment growth and job turnover, coupled with a declining number of graduates from special education teaching programs, are expected to result in a favorable job market for special education teachers.

Positions in rural areas and inner cities are more plentiful than job openings in suburban or wealthy urban areas. Also, job opportunities may be better in certain specialties—such as multiple disabilities, mental retardation, visual impairment, learning disabilities, and preschool special education—due to the considerable shortages of teachers in these fields. Special education teachers who are bilingual or have multicultural experience are also needed to work with an increasingly diverse student population.

Earnings

Salaries of special education teachers generally follow the same scale as those for general education teachers. According to the National Education Association, the estimated average salary of all public elementary and secondary school teachers in the 1995–96 school year was $37,900. Public secondary school teachers averaged about $38,600 a year, while public elementary school teachers averaged $37,300.

The Passion Factor: What do you like most about your occupation?

"I am very happy with my job," says Ester Rosales, a bilingual learning disabilities teacher who works in a large public school system. "I enjoy it because there is much more communication with the parents [than in regular classes]."

Rosales, who was born in Cuba, was already a bilingual teacher before she chose to specialize. "Our school needed special education teachers but we didn't have a program. I like working with students who have difficulties. They seem to do better when they get my attention."

Related Occupations

Other professionals whose occupation requires similar skills are school psychologists, social workers, speech pathologists, rehabilitation counselors, adapted physical education teachers, and occupational, physical, creative arts, and recreational therapists.

Additional Information

> National Clearinghouse for Professions in Special Education
> Council for Exceptional Children
> 1920 Association Drive
> Reston, VA 22091

To learn more about the special education teacher certification and licensing requirements in your state, contact your state's department of education.

Social Services

Bilingual social workers, human services workers, recreation workers and residential counselors are needed in many urban areas—and increasingly in the surrounding suburban communities—to help individuals and families navigate this society's environment.

"But it is not enough to speak the language," warns Celeste Pea, a licensed clinical social worker. "You have to understand the cultural differences between Mexicans and Cubans, for example, between urban and rural settings, and professional versus blue collar jobs. You need to know how to work with people."

Social Workers

"Some families have enormous conflicts because their adolescent children have become much more acculturated than the parents," relates Elena Liberman, a psychologist who also has a doctorate in social work and offers family therapy through a public service agency.

The Job

Social workers, also called caseworkers, help individuals and families cope with mental illness and problems such as inadequate housing, unemployment, lack of job skills, financial mismanagement, serious illness, disability, substance abuse, unwanted pregnancy, or antisocial behavior. They also work with families who have serious conflicts, including those involving child or spousal abuse.

Social workers help clients through direct counseling. Often, they provide concrete information such as where to go for debt counseling, how to find child care or elder care, how to apply for public assistance or other benefits, or how to get an alcoholic or drug addict admitted to a rehabilitation program. Social workers may also arrange for services in consultation with clients and then follow through to make sure the services are actually helpful. They may review eligibility requirements, fill out forms and applications, arrange for services, visit clients on a regular basis, and provide support during crises.

The majority of social workers specialize in a clinical field such as child welfare and family services, mental health, or school social work. **Clinical social workers** offer psychotherapy or counseling and a range of services in public agencies, clinics, as well as in private practice. Other social workers are employed in community organizations, administration, or research.

Child welfare workers or **family services workers** may counsel children and youths who have difficulty adjusting socially, advise parents on how to care for disabled children, or arrange for homemaker services during a parent's illness. Some social workers assist single parents, arrange adoptions, and help find foster homes for neglected, abandoned, or abused children or counsel at-risk families to avoid further abuse and neglect. Child welfare workers also work in residential institutions for children and adolescents.

Child or **adult protective services social workers** investigate reports of abuse and neglect and intervene if necessary. They may institute legal action to remove children from homes and place them temporarily in an emergency shelter or with a foster family.

Mental health social workers provide services for persons with mental or emotional problems, such as individual and group therapy, outreach, crisis intervention, social rehabilitation, and training in skills of everyday living.

Health care social workers help patients and their families cope with chronic, acute, or terminal illnesses and handle problems that may stand in the way of recovery or rehabilitation. They may organize support groups for families of patients suffering from cancer, AIDS, Alzheimer's disease, or other illnesses. They also advise family caregivers, counsel patients, and help plan for their needs after hospital discharge by arranging for at-home services from meals-on-wheels to oxygen equipment.

School social workers diagnose students' problems and arrange needed services, counsel children in trouble, and help integrate disabled and at-risk students into the general school population. School social workers deal with problems such as student pregnancy, misbehavior in class, and excessive absences. They also advise teachers on how to deal with problem students.

Social workers also focus on policy and planning. They help develop programs to address such issues as child abuse, homelessness, substance abuse, poverty, and violence. These workers research and analyze policies, programs, and regulations. They identify social problems and suggest legislative and other solutions.

Criminal justice social workers make recommendations to courts, do pre-sentencing assessments, and provide services for prison inmates and their families. **Probation** and **parole officers** provide similar services to individuals sentenced by a court to parole or probation.

Occupational social workers generally work in a corporation's personnel department or health unit. Through employee assistance programs, they help workers cope with job-related pressures or personal problems that affect the quality of their work. They offer direct counseling to employees, often those whose performance is hindered by emotional or family problems or substance abuse. They also develop education programs and refer workers to specialized community programs.

Some social workers specialize in gerontological services. They run support groups for family caregivers or for the adult children of aging parents; advise elderly people or family members about the choices in such areas as housing, transportation, and long-term care; and coordinate and monitor services.

According to the Bureau of Labor Statistics, social workers held about 585,000 jobs in 1996. Nearly 40 percent of the jobs were in state, county, or municipal government agencies, primarily in departments of human resources, social services, child welfare, mental health, health, housing, education, and corrections. Most social workers in the private sector were in voluntary social service agencies, community and religious organizations, hospitals, nursing homes, or home health agencies.

Education/Training

Most positions require at least a bachelor's degree. Small community agencies will hire undergraduate majors in psychology, sociology, and related fields in addition to the bachelor's in social work (BSW). A master's degree in social work (MSW) is generally necessary for positions in health and mental health settings. Jobs in public agencies may also require an MSW. Supervisory, administrative, and staff training positions usually require at least an MSW. College and university teaching positions and most research appointments normally require a doctorate in social work.

An MSW degree prepares graduates to perform assessments, manage cases, and supervise other workers. Master's programs usually last two years and include 900 hours of supervised field instruction, or internship. Entry into an MSW program does not require a bachelor's in social work, but courses in psychology, biology, sociology, economics, political science, history, social anthropology, urban studies, and social work are recommended. Some schools offer an accelerated MSW program for those with a BSW.

Career Mobility

Social workers may advance to supervisor, program manager, assistant director, or executive director of an agency or department. Advancement generally requires an MSW, as well as experience. Although some social workers with a BSW may be promoted to these positions after gaining experience, some employers choose to hire managers directly from MSW programs that focus specifically on management. These graduates often have little work experience but have an understanding of management through their education and training. Other career options for social workers include teaching, research, and consulting. Some help formulate government policies by analyzing and advocating policy positions in government agencies, in research institutions, and on legislators' staffs.

Some social workers go into private practice. Most private practitioners are clinical social workers who provide psychotherapy, usually paid through health insurance. Private practitioners must have an MSW and a period of supervised work experience. A network of contacts for referrals is also essential.

Since 1993, all states and the District of Columbia have had licensing, certification, or registration laws regarding social work practice and the use of professional titles. Standards for licensing vary by state.

Desired Characteristics

Social workers should be emotionally mature, objective, and sensitive to people and their problems. They must be able to handle responsibility, work independently, and maintain good working relationships with clients and co-workers. Volunteer or paid jobs as a social work aide offer ways of testing one's interest in this field.

Job Outlook

The Bureau of Labor Statistics projects 277,000 job openings for social workers through the year 2006, due to growth and net replacements. Among the factors contributing to employment growth are the rapidly growing number of older people, who are more likely to need social services, and the rising crime and juvenile delinquency. In addition, demand for social workers will be spurred by an increasing concern about services for the mentally ill, the mentally retarded, AIDS patients, and individuals and families in crisis.

Projected employment growth among social workers in hospitals reflects the current greater emphasis on early discharge of patients who might need services and social supports when they leave the hospital. Employment growth in home health care services is also due to a large and growing number of people who have impairments or disabilities that make it difficult to live at home without some form of assistance.

Opportunities for social workers in private practice will expand because of the anticipated availability of funding from health insurance and public-sector contracts. Also, with increasing affluence, people will be better able to pay for professional help to deal with personal problems. The growing popularity of employee assistance programs is also expected to spur demand for private practitioners, some of whom provide social work services to corporations on a contractual basis.

Employment of school social workers is expected to grow, due to expanded efforts to respond to the adjustment problems of immigrants, children from single-parent families, and rising rates of teen pregnancy. Moreover, continued emphasis on integrating disabled children into the general school population—a requirement under the Education for All Handicapped Children Act—will lead to more jobs.

Competition for social worker jobs is stronger in cities where training programs for social workers abound. Rural areas often find it difficult to attract and retain qualified staff.

Earnings

Based on limited information, the Bureau of Labor Statistics estimates that social workers with an MSW had median earnings of about $35,000 in 1997, while social workers with a BSW earned about $25,000.

According to a Hay Group survey of acute care hospitals, the median annual salary of full-time social workers with a master's degree was $35,000 in 1997. The middle 50 percent earned between $32,300 and $38,700.

The average annual salary for all social workers in the federal government in nonsupervisory, supervisory, and managerial positions was about $46,900 in 1997.

The Passion Factor: What do you like most about your occupation?

"It gives me great satisfaction to help people solve their problems," says psychologist and social worker Elena Liberman. "In this country, there are many Latinos who have very little access to mental health services. One of the reasons why this happens is because, in this field, we lack people who speak our language."

Born in Argentina, Liberman chose this profession because "I am very curious and I like to listen to people tell their life stories," she explained. "But I also thought I could help others feel better."

Related Occupations

Workers in occupations with similar duties include the clergy, counselors, counseling psychologists, and vocational rehabilitation counselors.

Additional Information

National Association of Social Workers
IC-Career Information
750 First Street NE, Suite 700
Washington, DC 20002-4241

National Network for Social Work Managers, Inc.
1316 New Hampshire Avenue NW, Suite 602
Washington, DC 20036

Council on Social Work Education
1600 Duke Street
Alexandria, VA 22314-3421

Government

Bilingual Latinos have an advantage in several occupations that fall within this category, all of which are expected to grow in the next decade. Firefighters, police, corrections officers, and security guards who work in Latino neighborhoods may find that speaking Spanish could mean the difference between life and death.

In this section, we will focus on urban and regional planners because their work can have a far-reaching impact on entire communities for years to come.

Urban and Regional Planners

"Being bilingual helps a lot," said Professor Curtis Winkle, director of the Urban Planning and Policy Department at the University of Illinois at Chicago. "Spanish comes in handy for an urban planner—not only in the international arena but also in [U.S.] cities where the Latino communities participate actively in the development process."

The Job

Urban and regional planners or city planners develop long and short-term land use plans to provide for growth and revitalization of urban, suburban, and rural communities, while helping local officials make decisions on social, economic, and environmental problems.

Planners devise plans promoting the most efficient use of a community's land and resources for residential, commercial, and recreational activities. They are involved in other planning activities, including social services, transportation, resource development, and the protection of ecologically sensitive regions.

Some of the issues planners address are traffic congestion, air pollution, and the effect of growth and change on a particular area. They also may formulate capital improvement plans for the construction of new school buildings, public housing, or sewage systems. Planners are involved in environmental issues ranging from pollution control to wetland preservation, forest conservation, and the location of new landfills. They also may be involved with drafting legislation on social issues such as the needs of the elderly, sheltering the homeless, or meeting the demand for new correctional facilities.

Planners also deal with land use and environmental issues created by population movements. For example, as suburban growth increases the need for traveling, some planners design new transportation systems and parking facilities.

Before preparing plans for community development, planners report on the current use of land for residential, business, and community purposes. These reports include information on the location of streets, highways, water and sewer lines, schools, libraries, and cultural and recreational sites, and provide data on the types of industries in the community, characteristics of the population, and employment and economic trends. With this information, along with input from citizens' advisory committees, planners design the layout of recommended buildings and other facilities such as subway lines and stations, and prepare reports that show how their programs can be carried out and what they will cost.

Planners increasingly use computers to record and analyze information and to prepare their reports and recommendations for government leaders and others.

In large organizations, planners usually specialize in a single area such as transportation, housing, historic preservation, urban design, environmental and regulatory issues, or economic development. In small organizations, planners must be generalists, able to do various kinds of planning.

According to the Bureau of Labor Statistics, urban and regional planners held about 29,000 jobs in 1996. About two out of three work for local governments. An increasing proportion of planners work in the private sector for companies involved with real estate and transportation. Others are employed in state agencies that deal with housing, transportation, or environmental protection, and a small number work for the federal government.

Many planners do consulting work, either part-time as a supplement to their regular jobs, or full-time. They provide services to private developers or government agencies. Private sector employers include architectural and surveying firms, management and public relations firms, educational institutions, large land developers, and law firms specializing in land use.

Education/Training

Most entry level jobs in federal, state, and local government agencies require a master's degree in urban or regional planning or urban design, or the equivalent in work experience. A bachelor's degree from an accredited planning program, coupled with a master's degree in architecture, landscape architecture, or civil engineering, is good preparation for entry-level planning jobs in areas such as urban design, traffic, or the environment.

A master's degree from an accredited planning program provides the best training for a number of planning fields. Although graduates from one of the limited number of accredited bachelor's degree programs qualify for many beginning positions, their advancement opportunities often are limited unless they acquire an advanced degree.

Familiarity with computer models and statistical techniques is necessary because of the increasing use of computerized modeling and geographic information systems in planning analyses.

In 1997, about eighty colleges and universities offered an accredited master's degree program, and about ten offered an accredited bachelor's degree program in urban or regional planning. These programs are accredited by the Planning Accreditation Board, which consists of representatives of the American Institute of Certified Planners, the American Planning Association, and the Association of Collegiate Schools of Planning. Most graduate programs in planning require a minimum of two years.

Specializations most commonly offered by planning schools are environmental planning, land use and comprehensive planning, economic development, and housing. Other popular offerings include community development, transportation, and urban design. Graduate students spend considerable time in studios, workshops, and laboratory courses.

Career Mobility

After acquiring a few years of experience, planners may advance to assignments requiring a high degree of independent judgment, such as designing the physical layout of a large development. Some public sector planners are promoted to jobs as planning directors and spend a great deal of time meeting with officials, speaking to civic groups, and supervising a staff. Further advancement occurs through a transfer to a larger jurisdiction with more complex problems and greater responsibilities, or into related occupations, such as director of community or economic development. In the private sector, experience leads to increases in independence and compensation.

Desired Characteristics

Planners must be able to think in terms of spatial relationships and visualize the effects of their plans and designs. They should be flexible and able to reconcile different viewpoints and to make constructive policy recommendations. The ability to communicate effectively, both orally and in writing, is necessary for anyone interested in this field.

Job Outlook

The Bureau of Labor Statistics projects the need for 6,000 urban and regional planners through the year 2006, due to growth and net replacements. Specific factors contributing to job growth include the need to regulate commercial development of suburban areas with rapidly growing populations and legislation related to issues of the environment, transportation, housing, and land use and development.

Movements such as historic preservation and central city redevelopment will provide additional openings for planners. However, local communities have limited resources and many demands for services.

Most new jobs for urban and regional planners will arise in rapidly expanding communities. Local governments need planners to address an array of problems associated with population growth. For example, new housing developments require roads, sewer systems, fire stations, schools, libraries, and recreation facilities that must be planned while considering budgetary constraints. Small town chambers of commerce, economic development authorities, and tourism bureaus are eager to hire planners, provided that the candidate has some background in marketing and public relations.

A master's degree from an accredited planning program, or a master's degree in civil engineering or landscape architecture coupled with training in transportation, environmental planning, geographic information systems, or urban design provide the most marketable background.

Earnings

Salaries of planners vary by educational attainment, type of employer, experience, size of community in which they work, and geographic location. According to a report by the American Planning Association (APA), in 1995, urban and regional planners with less than five years' experience earned median annual salaries of $30,000. Planners with between five and ten years' experience earned median salaries of $39,900. Those with more than ten years' experience earned median annual salaries of $55,000. The APA reports the median annual salary for all planners was $45,300. Salaries of community planners employed by the federal government in nonsupervisory, supervisory, and managerial positions averaged about $57,620 a year in early 1997.

The Passion Factor: What do you like most about your occupation?

"What I like most about my profession is that we pull different elements together to revitalize a neighborhood," says John Parker, an urban planner in private practice. "I also like the fact that civic groups are involved in the identification of their own issues and opportunities, so that we can craft a collective vision to make a change."

Parker, whose father is a social worker, is convinced that "city planning was tailor-made for me. I fell in love with cities and their physical development when I was a young child."

Related Occupations

Other professionals whose work is similar to the work of planners include architects, landscape architects, city managers, civil engineers, environmental engineers, and geographers.

Additional Information

American Planning Association
Education Division
122 S. Michigan Avenue, Suite 1600
Chicago, IL 60630-6107

Professional Services Careers

The downsizing of American corporations led to the outsourcing trend which is expected to continue. As companies pared down the size of their staff, keeping primarily groups of core employees, they began to contract out for services they needed but no longer had in-house. These services include public relations specialists, marketers and advertisers, human resources specialists, and lawyers. In response to that trend, many of those professionals have become consultants, who in turn hire other individuals—such as writers, artists, researchers, and paralegals—either as employees or freelancers.

While competition for all of these occupations is always keen, all are projected to remain strong prospects in the next decade. That is because many of these professionals, such as writers, visual artists, and marketing and public relations specialists, have skills that are needed more than ever because of the new technology. It is also because more and more companies are realizing the size and potential of the U.S. Latino market in addition to the Latin American markets and they need people who can help market their products and services in our communities. Thus, the following occupations offer some of the best opportunities for Latinos.

Public Relations Specialists

Bilingual public relations specialists are needed in U.S. companies that market products overseas and domestically. They also are needed in international companies, and are considered an asset by the governments of countries that are trying to create an identity in the U.S.

The Job

Public relations specialists advocate on behalf of organizations, and develop positive relationships with the public. Their role includes such functions as media, community, consumer, and governmental relations; political campaigns; or employee and investor relations. An important part of their job is to understand the attitudes and concerns of consumers, employees, and the various other "publics" the organization may have, and to establish and maintain cooperative relationships with their representatives.

Public relations specialists assemble information that raises awareness of an organization's policies, activities, and accomplishments among the general public, interest groups, and stockholders. Their work keeps management abreast of the public attitudes and concerns of its target audiences.

These professionals write and send press releases to the media, usually describing an organization's policies toward an issue or event. Their stories often become the seed for many radio or television special reports, newspaper stories, and magazine articles.

Public relations specialists also organize programs aimed at creating and maintaining contact between organization representatives and the public. These may include setting up speaking engagements, for which they might write the speeches for company officials. They also function as the company's representatives at community events or projects. In addition, they are responsible for preparing annual reports and writing proposals for various projects.

When public relations specialists work for government entities, they may be called **press secretaries**, **information officers**, **public affairs specialists**, or **communications specialists**. Their job is to keep the public informed about the activities of government agencies and officials. For example, a press secretary for a member of Congress tells constituents about the accomplishments of their elected representative.

In large organizations, the key public relations executive is often a vice president, who may develop overall plans and policies with other executives. People who serve as public relations specialists for individuals or small organizations may handle all aspects of the job.

According to the Bureau of Labor Statistics, public relations specialists held about 110,000 jobs in 1996. About two-thirds worked in service industries such as management and public relations firms, educational institutions, membership organizations, health care organizations, social service agencies, and advertising agencies. Others work for a wide range of employers, including manufacturing firms, financial institutions, and government agencies. Some are self-employed.

Public relations specialists tend to concentrate in large cities—such as New York, Los Angeles, Chicago, and Washington, DC, where press services and other communications facilities are readily available, and where many businesses and trade associations have their headquarters.

Education/Training

A college degree combined with public relations experience is an excellent foundation for public relations work. The ability to write and speak well is essential. Beginners typically have a college major in public relations, journalism, advertising, or communications. Some employers seek applicants with communications skills and training or experience in a field related to the firm's business, such as engineering or sales.

There are more than 200 colleges and about 100 graduate schools offering degree programs or special curricula in public relations, usually in a journalism or communications department. In addition, many other colleges offer at least one course in this field. Specialties are offered in public relations for business, government, or nonprofit organizations.

Many colleges help students obtain internships in public relations. A portfolio of published articles, television or radio programs, slide presentations, and other work is an asset in finding a job. Writing for a school publication or television or radio station provides valuable experience and material for one's portfolio.

Large public relations organizations, which tend to be more specialized, often have formal training programs for new employees. In smaller organizations, new employees work under the guidance of experienced staff members and generally get all-around experience.

Public relations specialists who meet prescribed requirements may receive accreditation from the Public Relations Society of America and the International Association of Business Communicators. Employers consider professional recognition through accreditation a sign of competence in this field, and it may be especially helpful in a competitive job market.

Career Mobility

Public relations specialists with demonstrated ability may be promoted to supervisory positions. Typical career paths in public relations firms start with research assistants or account assistants and advance to account executives, account supervisors, vice presidents, and eventually senior vice president. Although the titles may differ, a similar path is followed in corporate public relations. Some public relations specialists start their own consulting firms.

Desired Characteristics

Public relations specialists must have an outgoing personality, self-confidence, an understanding of human psychology, and an enthusiasm for motivating people. Also essential are creativity, initiative, good judgment, and the ability to express thoughts clearly, both orally and in writing.

Job Outlook

The Bureau of Labor Statistics projects that there will be 69,000 job openings for public relations specialists through the year 2006, due to growth and net replacements. Demand for public relations specialists will stem from the recognition that, in an increasingly competitive business environment, organizations of all sizes need good public relations.

Employment in public relations firms should grow as firms hire contractors to provide public relations services rather than support full-time staff. However, competition will be keen among recent college graduates with a degree in communications, journalism, public relations, advertising, or a related field. People without the appropriate educational background or work experience will face the toughest obstacles in trying to find a public relations job.

Earnings

The Bureau of Labor Statistics reports that the median annual earnings for salaried public relations specialists who usually worked full-time were about $34,000 in 1996. The middle 50 percent earned between $25,000 and $54,000 annually; the lowest 10 percent earned less than $16,000, and the top 10 percent earned more than $75,000.

According to a 1995 salary survey conducted for the Public Relations Society of America, the overall median salary in public relations was $49,070. Salaries in public relations ranged from less than $15,000 to more than $150,000. There was little difference between the median salaries in public relations firms and corporations, $51,340 and $50,770, respectively. However, practitioners working for government, health care, or nonprofit organizations had a considerably lower median salary of $43,260.

Public affairs specialists in the federal government in nonsupervisory, supervisory, and managerial positions averaged about $52,540 a year in 1996.

The Passion Factor: What do you like most about your occupation?

"It is very satisfying to shape a company's image and to see the desired results," says Rosa Carreras, who is in charge of media and promotions at a small public relations firm. "It isn't easy to do," she adds. "But it is precisely the challenge that always keeps me interested in my job."

Born in Colombia, Carreras was attracted to the communications field since she was very young. "I liked to create images or invent names and do something unusual with those concepts."

Related Occupations

Other professionals whose occupation requires similar skills include fund-raisers, lobbyists, promotion managers, advertising managers, and police officers involved in community relations.

Additional Information

Public Relations Society of America, Inc.
33 Irving Place
New York, NY 10003-2376

PR Reporter
PO Box 600
Exeter, NH 03833

The American Society for Health Care Marketing and
    Public Relations
American Hospital Association
One N. Franklin Street
Chicago, IL 60606

Marketing, Advertising, and Public Relations Managers

These professionals and their staffs often can make the difference between the success or failure of an organization. Without advertising, the intended target public would not know that a product exists. Without marketing efforts, the product could not reach the intended consumer. And, without public relations, a company might loose touch with its markets and allow its products to become obsolete.

The expertise of these professionals is now considered key in every industry. For example, banks and credit unions, once considered stodgy, bureaucratic institutions, are now using marketing principles to attract customers to their new financial products. And, as discussed earlier, even to sell products or services through the Internet, businesses must know something about marketing, advertising, and public relations. If you can do all of this in Spanish, and/or are familiar with the Latino market, this is a field you should explore.

The Job

The main goal of any company is to market its products or services in a profitable way. Depending on the size of the firm, marketing responsibilities may be assumed by one person, such as the owner or chief executive officer, or they may be shared by a number of professionals with expertise in marketing, advertising, and public relations.

In large firms, the executive vice president for marketing directs the overall marketing policy, including market research, marketing strategy, sales, advertising, promotion, pricing, product development, and public relations activities. In turn, all these activities are supervised by middle and supervisory managers who oversee staffs of professionals and technicians.

Marketing managers are responsible for developing the company's marketing strategy. They work with a variety of subordinates, including product development managers and market research managers, to determine the demand for products and services offered by the firm and its competitors and identify potential consumers. Marketing managers also develop pricing strategies that can maximize the firm's share of the market and its profits. With a team of sales, product development, and other managers, they monitor trends that indicate the need for new products and services and oversee product development. Marketing managers work with advertising and promotion managers to find the most effective methods to promote the firm's products and services and to attract potential users.

Sales managers are in charge of the company's sales program. Their job is to establish goals, assign sales territories, and oversee any local or regional sales managers. Sales managers also analyze the company's sales statistics in order to determine sales potential and inventory needs, and stay abreast of the customers' preferences.

In large firms, **advertising managers** oversee the account services, creative services, and media services departments. **Account executives** manage the account services department. They evaluate the need for advertising and, in advertising agencies, maintain the clients' accounts. It is up to the **creative services department** to develop the subject matter and presentation of advertising. The **media services department** selects the communication media that will carry the advertising message.

In smaller companies, advertising and promotion staffs tend to be made up of just a few people who serve as a liaison between the firm and the advertising or promotion agency to which many of those functions are contracted out.

Promotion managers are responsible for promotion programs which combine advertising with purchase incentives to increase sales of products or services. Promotion programs, which are aimed at establishing closer contact with purchasers-dealers, distributors, or consumers, may involve direct mail, telemarketing, television or radio advertising, catalogs, exhibits, inserts in newspapers, in-store displays and product endorsements, and special events. Purchase incentives may include discounts, samples, gifts, rebates, coupons, sweepstakes, and contests.

Public relations managers supervise public relations specialists. These managers direct publicity programs to a targeted public, using any necessary communication media to maintain their support. The success of their organization depends on such groups, which may include consumers, stockholders, or the general public. They assess the compatibility of advertising and promotion programs with public relations efforts. Public relations managers play a key role for top management. They observe social, economic, and political trends that might affect the firm and make recommendations to strengthen the firm's public image in view of those trends. Public relations managers may work with labor relations managers to produce internal company communications, such as a newsletter about employee-management relations, and with financial managers to produce company reports. They assist company executives in drafting speeches, arranging interviews, and responding to information requests. In addition, some public relations managers handle special events.

According to the Bureau of Labor Statistics, marketing, advertising, and public relations managers held about 482,000 jobs in 1996. While they worked in virtually every industry, a significant number of these professionals worked in printing and publishing firms, advertising agencies, department stores, computer and data processing services firms, and management and public relations firms.

Education/Training

Most employers prefer applicants with a broad liberal arts background for entry into marketing, advertising, and public relations managerial positions. But many other educational backgrounds are suitable for these professions. A bachelor's degree in sociology, psychology, literature, or philosophy, among other subjects, is acceptable.

For marketing, sales, and promotion management positions, some employers prefer a bachelor's or master's degree in business administration with an emphasis on marketing. In highly technical industries, such as computer and electronics manufacturing, a bachelor's degree in engineering or science combined with a master's degree in business administration is preferred.

For advertising management positions, some employers prefer a bachelor's degree in advertising or journalism. For public relations management positions, some employers prefer a bachelor's or master's degree in public relations or journalism. For all these specialties, courses in management and completion of an internship while in school are highly recommended. Familiarity with computerized word processing and database applications also are important for many marketing, advertising, and public relations management positions.

Career Mobility

Most marketing, advertising, and public relations management positions are filled by promoting experienced staff or related professional or technical workers. Promotions are likely to occur much faster in large firms. Although experience, ability, and leadership are emphasized for promotion, advancement can be accelerated by participation in management training programs. Many firms also provide their employees with continuing education opportunities and encourage employee participation in seminars and conferences, which are often provided by professional societies.

Marketing, advertising, and public relations managers often are prime candidates for advancement because of the importance and high visibility of their jobs. Well-trained, experienced, successful managers may be promoted to higher positions in their own or other firms. Some become top executives. Managers with extensive experience and sufficient capital may open their own businesses.

Desired Characteristics

Marketing, advertising, and public relations managers should be mature, creative, and highly motivated. They must be able to communicate persuasively, both orally and in writing, with other managers, staff, and the public. These professionals also need to have tact, display good judgment, and exceptional ability to establish and maintain effective personal relationships with supervisory and professional staff members and client firms.

Job Outlook

The Bureau of Labor Statistics projects that there will be 226,000 jobs for marketing, advertising and public relations managers through the year 2006, due to growth and net replacements. These positions are highly coveted and competition is fierce.

Employment growth will be driven by increasingly intense domestic and global competition in products and services offered to consumers, which will necessitate greater marketing, promotional, and public relations efforts. Management and public relations firms may experience particularly rapid growth as businesses increasingly hire contractors for these services rather than support additional full-time staff.

Employment of marketing, advertising, and public relations managers is expected to grow much faster than average in most business services industries, such as computer and data processing, and management and public relations firms. However, only average growth is projected in manufacturing industries overall. Many companies that eliminated in-house marketing and advertising departments during downsizing in recent years are now relying on firms which specialize in promotion, marketing, and advertising activities to provide these services.

Earnings

According to a National Association of Colleges and Employers survey, starting salaries for marketing majors graduating in 1997 averaged about $29,000; advertising majors, about $27,000.

The median annual salary of marketing, advertising, and public relations managers was $46,000 in 1996. The lowest 10 percent earned $23,000 or less, while the top 10 percent earned $97,000 or more. Many earn bonuses equal to 10 percent or more of their salaries. Surveys show that salary levels vary substantially depending upon the level of managerial responsibility, length of service, education, and the employer's size, location, and industry. For example, manufacturing firms generally pay marketing, advertising, and public relations managers higher salaries than nonmanufacturing firms. For sales managers, the size of their sales territory is another important determinant of salary.

According to a 1996 survey by *Advertising Age*, the average annual salary of a vice president brand manager was $79,000; vice president product manager, $105,000; vice president advertising, $130,000; and vice president marketing, $133,000.

According to a 1996 survey by the Public Relations Society of America, senior public relations managers earned an average of $76,790.

The Passion Factor: What do you like most about your occupation?

"The first time I worked on an advertising campaign, back in college, I realized it was a tremendous challenge," recalls Beatriz Ramírez, an account executive in a large advertising firm. "I knew then that it involved much more than an idea, that I had to do research, work with other creative people, and know how to tell the client what I wanted to do. I still get the same sense of excitement when we begin to develop a new campaign."

Related Occupations

Other personnel involved with marketing, advertising, and public relations include art directors, commercial and graphic artists, copy chiefs, copywriters, editors, lobbyists, market research analysts, public relations specialists, promotion specialists, sales representatives, and technical writers.

Additional Information

American Marketing Association
250 S. Wacker Drive
Chicago, IL 60606

American Advertising Federation
Education Services Department
1101 Vermont Avenue NW
Suite 500
Washington, DC 20005

Sales and Marketing Executives International
458 Statler Office Tower
Cleveland, OH 44115

Council of Sales Promotion Agencies
750 Summer Street
Stamford, CT 06901

Promotion Marketing Association of America, Inc.
322 Eighth Avenue
Suite 1201
New York, NY 10001

Writers and Editors

Writers and editors communicate through words. Whether they write for the printed page, an on-line service, a movie screen, or the air waves, their skills will always be needed and can be applied to any field. Those writers who are bilingual continue to find outlets for their craft, as the number of Spanish-language or bilingual publications and radio and television stations remains stable or grows.

The Job

The written word is the tool of the trade for writers and editors. Writers may write fiction and nonfiction books; articles for magazines, trade journals, newspapers, and company newsletters; pieces for radio and television broadcasts; scripts for movies; technical reports; and advertising copy. Editors select and prepare material for publication or broadcasting and supervise writers.

Specialties include **newswriters**, who prepare news items for newspapers or news broadcasts; **columnists**, who analyze news and write commentaries; **editorial writers**, who write comments to stimulate or mold public opinion; and **reporters** and **correspondents**, who may also write articles or copy for broadcast.

Technical writers make scientific and technical information easy to understand for nontechnical audiences. They prepare operating and maintenance manuals, catalogs, parts lists, assembly instructions, sales promotion materials, and project proposals. They also plan and edit technical reports and oversee preparation of illustrations, photographs, diagrams, and charts.

Copywriters write advertising copy to promote the sale of goods and services. Others may work as **freelance writers**, selling their work to publishers, public relations and advertising agencies, and other firms.

Editors review, rewrite, and edit the work of writers. However, their primary duties are to plan the contents of books, magazines, or newspapers and to supervise their preparation. In small organizations, a single editor may do everything. In larger ones, an **executive editor** oversees **associate** or **assistant editors** who have responsibility for particular subjects, such as fiction, or international news. Editors also hire writers, reporters, or other employees; plan budgets; and negotiate contracts with freelance writers. In broadcasting companies, **program directors** have similar responsibilities.

According to the Bureau of Labor Statistics, writers and editors held about 286,000 jobs in 1996. Nearly a third of salaried writers and editors worked for newspapers, magazines, and book publishers. Substantial numbers also worked in advertising agencies, in radio and television broadcasting, in public relations firms, and on journals and newsletters published by business and nonprofit organizations, such as professional associations, labor unions, and religious organizations. Others developed publications for government agencies or wrote for motion picture companies.

Many technical writers work for computer software firms or manufacturers of aircraft, chemicals, pharmaceuticals, and computers and other electronic equipment.

Thousands of other individuals work as freelancers, earning some income from their articles, books, and less commonly, television and movie scripts. Most supplement their needs with income derived from other sources.

Education/Training

Most employers like to hire writers or editors with a college degree, preferably in communications, journalism, or English. However, some employers look for a broad liberal arts background.

Technical writing requires a degree in, or some knowledge about a specialized field such as engineering, business, or one of the sciences. Often, people with good writing skills obtain the specialized knowledge on the job. Some transfer from jobs as technicians, scientists, or engineers. Others begin as research assistants, editorial assistants, or trainees in a technical information department, develop technical communication skills, and then assume writing duties.

Career Mobility

In small firms, writers and editors may start as editorial or production assistants, and begin to write or edit material right away. They often advance by moving to other firms. In larger firms, where jobs tend to be more formally structured, beginners generally do research, check facts, or edit copy. They take on full-scale writing or editing duties less rapidly than do the employees of small companies. Advancement comes as they are assigned more important articles.

Desired Characteristics

Writers and editors must be able to express ideas clearly and logically, and should have a broad range of knowledge. They should be creative and curious, self-motivated, and persistent. Increasingly, they need to be familiar with electronic publishing, graphics, and video production equipment. On-line newspapers and magazines require knowledge of computer software used to combine on-line text with graphics, audio, video, and 3-D animation.

Editors must have the good judgment necessary to decide what material to accept and which to reject. They need tact and the ability to guide and encourage others in their work.

Job Outlook

The Bureau of Labor Statistics projects that there will be 124,000 jobs for writers and editors through the year 2006 due to growth and net replacements. Demand for technical writers will be spurred by the continuing expansion of scientific and technical information, and the continued need to communicate it. As well, opportunities will be good in this specialty because fewer writers can handle technical material.

On-line publications and services, which are relatively new, will continue to grow and require an increased number of writers and editors.

Employment of salaried writers and editors by newspapers, periodicals, book publishers, and nonprofit organizations is expected to increase with growing demand for their publications. Growth of advertising and public relations agencies should also be a source of new jobs.

Earnings

In 1996, beginning salaries for writers and editorial assistants averaged $21,000 annually, according to the Dow Jones Newspaper Fund. According to the Newspaper Guild those who had at least five years of experience averaged more than $30,000 and senior editors at the largest newspapers earned over $67,000 a year.

According to the 1996 Technical Communicator's Salary Survey, the median annual salary for technical writers was $44,000.

The average annual salary for technical writers and editors in the federal government in nonsupervisory, supervisory, and managerial positions was about $47,440 in 1996; other writers and editors averaged about $46,590.

The Passion Factor: What do you like most about your occupation?

"It always makes me feel good when one of my readers tells me that my ideas are helpful," says Gabriela Moran, a consumer columnist who works for a suburban weekly. "It is important to me that my work makes a difference in other people's lives."

Related Occupations

Other jobs that require similar skills include newspaper reporters and correspondents, radio and television announcers, advertising and public relations workers, and teachers.

Additional Information

The Dow Jones Newspaper Fund
PO Box 300
Princeton, NJ 08540

American Society of Magazine Editors
919 Third Avenue
New York, NY 10022

National Association of Hispanic Journalists
1193 National Press Building
Washington, DC 20045
(202) 662-7145
http://www.nahj.org

Society for Technical Communication, Inc.
901 N. Stuart Street, Suite 904
Arlington, VA 22203

The Newspaper Guild
Research and Information Department
8611 Second Avenue
Silver Spring, MD 20910

National Newspaper Association
1525 Wilson Boulevard, Suite 550
Arlington, VA 22209

Visual Artists

Visual artists communicate through graphic images and symbols. Whether they create designs for the printed page, on-line services, movie screens, or television, their skills will always be needed and can be applied to any field. Those artists who are bicultural can express the needs and views of their employers or clients who want to reach other nations—perhaps through the Internet. If they also are bilingual, they add double value to their craft.

The Job

Graphic artists, whether freelancers or employed by a firm, work for commercial clients, such as major corporations, retail stores, and advertising, design, or publishing firms. Using a variety of print, electronic, and film media, they may create promotional displays and marketing brochures for new products, visual designs of annual reports and other corporate literature, or distinctive logos for products or businesses. Artists may be responsible for the overall layout and design of magazines, newspapers, journals, and other publications, and may create graphics for television and computer-generated media. For example, many magazines and newspapers have a homepage on the Internet.

Illustrators paint, draw, or electronically create pictures for books, magazines, and other publications; films; and paper products, including greeting cards, calendars, wrapping paper, and stationery. Many do a variety of illustrations, while others specialize in a particular style. Some illustrators draw storyboards for television commercials, movies, and animated features. Storyboards present television commercials in a series of scenes similar to a comic strip, so an advertising agency and client can evaluate proposed commercials. Some work is produced or delivered electronically, using computer software and hardware such as scanners. This allows ideas to be electronically mailed between clients, or presented on the Internet.

Medical and scientific illustrators combine artistic skills with knowledge of the biological sciences. Medical illustrators draw illustrations of human anatomy and surgical procedures. Scientific illustrators draw illustrations of animals and plants. These illustrations are used in publications, and in audiovisual presentations for teaching purposes. Medical illustrators also work for lawyers, producing exhibits for court cases. **Fashion artists** draw illustrations of women's, men's, and children's clothing and accessories for newspapers, magazines, and other media.

Art directors, also called **visual journalists**, read the material to be printed in periodicals, newspapers, and other printed media, and decide how to best present visually the information in an eye-catching and organized manner. They make decisions about which photographs or art work to use, and oversee production of the printed material. Art directors may also review graphics that will be shown on the Internet.

According to the Bureau of Labor Statistics, visual artists held about 276,000 jobs in 1996. Nearly six out of ten were self-employed and made their living as freelancers. Of the artists who were not self-employed, many were graphic artists who worked for advertising agencies, design firms, commercial art and reproduction firms, or printing and publishing firms. Other artists were employed by the motion picture and television industries, wholesale and retail trade establishments, and public relations firms.

Education/Training

In the graphic arts field, demonstrated artistic ability, appropriate training, or other qualifications are needed for success. Evidence of appropriate talent and skill, displayed in an artist's portfolio, is an important factor used by art and design directors and others in deciding whether to hire or contract out work to an artist. To assemble their portfolio, most artists participate in a bachelor's degree program or other post-secondary training in art, design, or visual communications. Internships also provide excellent opportunities for artists to develop and enhance their portfolios. Formal educational programs in art and design also provide training in computer design techniques; computers are widely used in art and design, and knowledge and training in computer techniques are critical for many jobs in these fields.

According to the American Institute of Graphic Arts, more than ninety percent of artists have a college degree; among this group, over six out of ten majored in graphic design and nearly two out of ten majored in fine arts.

Medical illustrators must demonstrate artistic ability, and also must have a detailed knowledge of living organisms, surgical and medical procedures, and human and sometimes animal anatomy. A four-year bachelor's degree combining art and premedical courses is usually required, followed by a master's degree in medical illustration. This degree is offered in only a few accredited schools in the United States.

Career Mobility

Graphic artists may advance to assistant art director, art director, design director, and in some companies, creative director of an art or design department. Some artists eventually become successful freelancers or prefer to specialize in a particular area. Some graphic artists become webmasters, maintaining their company's Internet site. Others decide to open their own businesses. Fine artists and illustrators advance as their work circulates, and as they establish a reputation for a particular style.

Desired Characteristics

Persons hired in advertising agencies or graphic design studios often start with relatively routine work. Others have enough talent, perseverance, and confidence in their ability to start out freelancing full-time immediately after graduating from art school. The freelance artist develops a set of clients who regularly contract for work. Some successful freelancers are widely recognized for their skill in specialties, such as children's book illustration, design, or magazine illustration. These artists may earn high incomes and can pick and choose the type of work they do.

Job Outlook

The Bureau of Labor Statistics projects that there will be 135,000 jobs for artists and commercial artists through the year 2006, due to growth and net replacements. Demand will rise as producers of information, goods, and services place increasing emphasis on visual appeal in product design, advertising, marketing, and television. The explosive growth of the Internet is expected to provide many additional opportunities for graphic artists.

Graphic arts studios, galleries, and individual clients are always on the lookout for artists who display outstanding talent, creativity, and style. Talented artists who have developed a mastery of artistic techniques and skills, including computer skills, will have the best job prospects.

Earnings

According to the Bureau of Labor Statistics, median earnings for salaried visual artists who usually work full-time were about $27,100 a year in 1996. The middle 50 percent earned between $20,000 and $36,400 a year. The top 10 percent earned more than $43,000, and the bottom 10 percent earned less than $15,000.

The Society of Publication Designers estimates that entry-level graphic designers earned between $23,000 and $27,000 annually in 1997.

Earnings for self-employed visual artists vary widely. Well-established freelancers and fine artists may earn much more than salaried artists.

The Passion Factor: What do you like most about your occupation?

"What I like most about my work is the interaction with my clients and the flexibility it gives me," says Aurelio Campos, a self-employed graphic designer who became interested in the field after he took a course in typography more than ten years ago. "It grew on me and I kept taking courses—illustration, paste-up, and computerized design. Then I was hired by McDonald's and later by a catalogue company. Once I had a portfolio, I was able to branch out on my own."

Related Occupations

Other jobs that require similar skills include architects, display workers, landscape architects, photographers, and floral, industrial, and interior designers. In addition, several occupational options associated with the Internet have emerged such as webmaster and Internet page designer. These jobs often require artistic talent as well as computer skills.

Additional Information

The National Association of Schools of Art and Design
11250 Roger Bacon Drive
Suite 21
Reston, VA 20190

The Association of Medical Illustrators
1819 Peachtree Street NE
Suite 712
Atlanta, GA 30309-1848

The American Institute of Graphic Arts
164 Fifth Avenue
New York, NY 10010

The Society of Publication Designers
60 E. 42nd Street
Suite 721
New York, NY 10165-1416

Human Resources Specialists and Managers

"The entire field of human resources has changed dramatically in the last decade," says Fran Daly, associate director of the WorkPlace Studies program at Loyola University in Chicago. "The change to human resources [from personnel] specialists, which took place at the beginning of the '90s signaled the difference in attitude," she continues. "Human resources professionals are no longer just clerical paper pushers. They have become strategic business partners who have a pipeline to the top of an organization."

The Job

Human resources specialists and managers—known in the past as **personnel**, **training**, and **labor relations specialists**—recruit and interview employees and advise top management on hiring decisions. They also help utilize the employees' skills effectively, provide training opportunities to enhance those skills, and boost employees' satisfaction with their jobs and working conditions.

If the organization is small, one person may be responsible for all aspects of human resources work. In a large corporation, the top human resources executive usually develops and coordinates personnel programs and policies which are implemented by a director or manager of human resources.

The human resources director may be in charge of several departments, each headed by an experienced manager, who most likely specializes in one personnel activity. **Employment** and **placement managers** are responsible for hiring and firing employees and supervise various workers, including equal employment opportunity specialists and recruitment specialists.

Recruiters screen, interview, and sometimes test applicants. They may also check references and make employment offers to qualified candidates. These professionals must be thoroughly familiar with the organization and its personnel policies to discuss wages, working conditions, and promotional opportunities with prospective employees. Recruiters may travel extensively—often to college campuses—to search for potential job candidates.

EEO representatives or **affirmative action coordinators** handle this area in large organizations. They investigate and resolve equal opportunity–related grievances, examine corporate practices for possible violations, and compile and submit EEO statistical reports.

Employer relations representatives usually work in government agencies and develop working relationships with local employers to promote the use of public employment programs and services. Similarly, **employment interviewers** (sometimes called **personnel consultants** or **human resources coordinators**) help match job seekers with employers.

Job analysts collect and examine detailed information about job duties to prepare job descriptions. **Occupational analysts** conduct research related to occupational classification systems and occupational trends.

Compensation managers establish and maintain a firm's pay system. In addition, they often oversee their firm's performance evaluation system, and may design reward systems such as pay-for-performance plans.

Employee benefits managers handle the company's employee benefits program, particularly its health insurance and pension plans. They must have expertise in the design and administration of benefits programs because employer-provided benefits account for a growing proportion of overall compensation costs. They also must be familiar with health benefits, an area that has become top priority as more firms struggle to cope with the rising cost of health care for employees and retirees. Some firms offer their employees life and accidental death-and-dismemberment insurance, disability insurance, and relatively new benefits designed to meet the needs of a changing workforce, such as parental leave, child care and elder care, long-term nursing home care insurance, employee assistance and wellness programs, and flexible benefits plans.

Management increasingly recognizes that training offers employees a way to develop skills, which enhances productivity and quality of work, and builds loyalty to the firm. **Training** and **development managers** supervise this function, now widely accepted as a method of improving employee morale. Other factors contributing to the growing importance of training include the complexity of the work environment, the rapid pace of organizational and technological change, and the ever-expanding number of jobs in fields that constantly generate new knowledge. Training specialists plan, organize, and direct a wide range of training activities. They conduct orientation sessions and arrange on-the-job training for new employees. They also help supervisors improve their interpersonal skills in order to deal effectively with employees and may set up individualized training plans to strengthen an employee's existing skills. In some companies, training specialists set up programs to develop executive potential among employees in lower-level positions.

The **director of industrial relations** develops labor policy, oversees industrial labor relations, negotiates collective bargaining agreements, and coordinates grievance procedures to handle complaints resulting from disputes under the contract for firms with unionized employees. However, because union membership is continuing to decline in most industries, industrial relations personnel are working more with employees who are not members of a labor union.

Dispute resolution specialists—that is, people who obtain agreement between conflicting parties—include **conciliators**, or **mediators** and **arbitrators**. Other emerging specialists include **international human resources managers**, who handle human resources issues related to a company's foreign operations, and **human resources information system specialists**, who develop and apply computer programs to process personnel information, match job seekers with job openings, and handle other personnel matters.

Human resources specialists are employed in virtually every industry. According to the Bureau of Labor Statistics, human resources specialists and managers held about 544,000 jobs in 1996. Specialists accounted for three out of five positions; managers, for two out of five. About 15,000 specialists were self-employed, working as consultants to public and private employers.

Among the professionals who have salaried jobs, 85 percent work in the private sector in services industries such as business, health, social, management, and educational services. Labor organizations account for one out of ten salaried human resources specialists; manufacturing industries account for two out of ten jobs, while finance, insurance, and real estate firms account for about one out of ten.

Education/Training

The educational backgrounds of human resources specialists vary widely. Most employers generally seek college graduates to fill entry-level positions. Some favor students who majored in human resources, personnel administration, or industrial and labor relations, while others prefer applicants with a liberal arts education. Other employers only consider candidates with business or technical backgrounds.

Many colleges and universities offer programs leading to one or more specialties in human relations. Because an interdisciplinary background is appropriate for this field, people may take courses in behavioral sciences or business. In some cases, a more targeted education in such fields as engineering, law, or finance is helpful. Knowledge of compensation, recruitment, training and development, and performance appraisal, as well as principles of management, organizational structure, and industrial psychology is essential.

Entry-level workers often receive on-the-job training where they learn such things as job classifications, interviewing techniques, and administration of benefits. Persons seeking general and top management positions should get a master's degree in human resources, labor relations, or business administration with a concentration in human resources. Experience is a must for any managerial position.

Career Mobility

Exceptional human resources workers may be promoted to director of human resources or industrial relations, which can eventually lead to top managerial or executive positions. Some may join consulting firms or open their own business. A PhD is an advantage for teaching, writing, and consulting work.

Desired Characteristics

These professionals should have excellent oral and written communications skills and the ability to work with or supervise people of all levels of education and experience. They must be patient, emotionally stable, and able to function under stress. Integrity and a persuasive, affable personality are good qualities.

Job Outlook

The Department of Labor projects that there will be 153,000 job openings for human resources specialists through the year 2006 due to growth and net replacements. Most new jobs for these professionals will be in the private sector, as employers, increasingly concerned about productivity and quality of work, devote greater resources to job-specific training programs in response to the growing complexity of many jobs, the aging of the workforce, and technological advances that can leave employees with obsolete skills. In addition, rising health care costs should spur demand for specialists to develop creative compensation and benefits packages that firms can offer prospective employees. Employment of labor relations staff, including arbitrators and mediators, should grow as firms become more involved in labor relations, and attempt to resolve potentially costly labor-management disputes out of court. Increasing demand for international human resources managers and human resources information systems specialists may spur additional job growth.

Employment demand should be strong in management and consulting firms and personnel supply firms as businesses in-

creasingly contract out human relations functions or hire personnel specialists on a contractual basis to meet the increasing cost
and complexity of training and development programs. Demand
should also increase in firms that develop and administer the increasingly complex employee benefits and compensation packages for other organizations.

Earnings

According to a salary survey conducted by the National Association of Colleges and Employers, bachelor's degree candidates ma-
joring in human resources, including labor relations, received
starting offers averaging $25,300 a year in 1996; master's degree
candidates, $39,900.

According to a 1996 survey of compensation in the human
resources field, conducted by Abbott, Langer, and Associates of
Crete, Illinois, the median total cash compensation for selected
personnel and labor relations occupations were:

Median Annual Salary for Selected Human Resources Personnel

Industrial/labor relations directors	$106,100
Divisional human resources directors	91,300
Compensation and benefits directors	90,500
Employee/community relations directors	87,500
Training and organizational directors	86,600
Benefits directors	80,500
Plant/location human resources managers	64,400
Recruitment and interviewing managers	63,800
Compensation supervisors	53,400
Training generalists	49,900
Employment interviewing supervisors	42,800
Safety specialists	42,500
Job evaluation specialists	39,600
Employee assistance/employee counseling specialists	39,000
Human resources information systems specialists	38,800
Benefits specialists	38,300
EEO/affirmative action specialists	38,200
Training material development specialists	37,200
Employee services/employee recreation specialists	35,000

Source: National Association of Colleges and Employers

According to a survey of workplaces in 160 metropolitan areas, personnel specialists with limited experience had median earnings of $25,700 a year in 1995, the middle half earned between $23,700 and $28,500 a year. Personnel supervisors/managers with limited experience had median earnings of $59,000 a year. The middle half earned between $54,000 and $65,200 a year.

In the federal government in 1997, persons with a bachelor's degree or three years of general experience in the personnel field generally started at $19,500 a year. Those with a superior academic record or an additional year of specialized experience started at $24,200 a year. Those with a master's degree may start at $29,600, and those with a doctorate in a personnel field may start at $35,800. Beginning salaries were slightly higher in areas where the prevailing local pay level was higher. There are no formal entry-level requirements for managerial positions. Personnel specialists in the federal government averaged $52,900 a year in 1997; personnel managers, $55,400.

The Passion Factor: What do you like most about your occupation?

"I like to look for areas in which we can support the development of an individual employee. In fact, I'm passionate about this," says Juan Fernández, manager of strategic staffing in emerging markets for a large manufacturing concern. "I am known as a seeker of corporate gold because I never get tired of interviewing people. Perhaps, among the eight or nine interviews I often conduct in one day, I might find an individual who could become a vice-president of the company in the future."

Related Occupations

Other professionals whose occupation requires similar skills include employment, rehabilitation, and college career planning and placement counselors; lawyers; psychologists; sociologists; social workers; public relations specialists; and teachers.

Additional Information

American Society for Training and Development
1640 King Street, Box 1443
Alexandria, VA 22313

American Compensation Association
14040 Northsight Boulevard
Scottsdale, AZ 85260

International Foundation of Employee Benefit Plans
18700 W. Bluemound Road
Brookfield, WI 53045

Industrial Relations Research Association
University of Wisconsin
7226 Social Science Building
1180 Observatory Drive
Madison, WI 53706

International Association of Personnel in Employment
    Security
1801 Louisville Road
Frankfort, KY 40601

Lawyers

If you are interested in law but have been discouraged by recent reports of an oversupply of these professionals, you should know that some of those rumors are true. There is a glut of lawyers in certain types of practices. And the large law firms, which have followed the downsizing trend, are no longer hiring as many graduates as they did in the eighties.

However, there are also poor people in this country who have no access to legal defense. Because they are disadvantaged, they have no legal representation when they need it. Public interest law, while not a lucrative practice, is an area that always needs attorneys.

"We also need attorneys who understand our language and culture," says Martin Castro, a partner at the law firm of Baker & McKenzie whose work involves commercial litigation, business disputes, and international law. "And we need them at all levels: in the community, in corporate boardrooms, and in Washington, writing and interpreting laws. The law profession affects the whole society."

Other specialty areas in law that show promise are bankruptcy, taxes, intellectual copyright, and practices that focus on the legal needs of the older population.

The Job

Lawyers, also called **attorneys**, interpret the law and apply it to specific situations. They either advocate for their clients in criminal and civil trials, or give them advice regarding their legal rights and obligations. Often, they do both.

In order to prepare a case, lawyers research the applicable laws and judicial decisions that have been applied to those laws under circumstances similar to those currently faced by the client. Today's lawyers supplement their law library research with computer software packages, which can automatically search legal literature and identify texts relevant to a specific case. **Tax lawyers** are increasingly using computers to compute taxes and explore alternative strategies for their clients. Based on the results of their research, attorneys can advise clients as to possible actions they may take and draw up legal documents, such as wills and contracts, for them.

Most lawyers choose a field of specialization. **Trial lawyers**, for example, spend much of their time outside the courtroom conducting research, interviewing clients and witnesses, and handling other details in preparation for trial. Other law specialties include bankruptcy, probate, or international law. **Environmental lawyers** may represent public interest groups, waste disposal companies, or construction firms when they deal with the Environmental Protection Agency (EPA) and other state and federal agencies.

Some lawyers concentrate in the emerging field of intellectual property, where they help protect clients' claims to copyrights, artwork under contract, product designs, and computer programs. Others advise insurance companies about their transactions. They also review claims filed against insurance companies and represent the companies in court.

The majority of lawyers concentrate on either criminal or civil law and work in private practice. In criminal law, they represent individuals who have been charged with crimes. In civil law, attorneys help clients with litigation, wills, trusts, contracts, mortgages, titles, and leases. Some manage a person's property as trustees or executors. Others accept only public interest cases—civil or criminal—which have the potential to impact many people beyond the individual client.

If a lawyer is employed by a single client, such as a corporation, this professional is known as **house counsel**. The job entails advising the firm about legal issues related to its business activities, such as patents, government regulations, contracts with other companies, property interests, or collective bargaining agreements with unions.

Another category of lawyers is made up by those who are employed at various levels of government. They help develop programs, draft laws, interpret legislation, establish enforcement procedures, and argue civil and criminal cases on behalf of the government. At the state level, attorneys who work for the attorney general, prosecutors, public defenders, and courts play a key role in the criminal justice system. At the federal level, lawyers investigate cases for the Department of Justice or other agencies.

Other lawyers work for legal aid societies—private, nonprofit organizations established to serve disadvantaged people. A relatively small number of trained attorneys work in law schools as faculty members. Some lawyers become judges, although not all judges have practiced law.

According to the Bureau of Labor Statistics, lawyers held about 622,000 jobs in 1996. About three-fourths of the practicing attorneys were in private practice, either in law firms or in solo practices. Other lawyers worked for the government, primarily at the local level. In the federal government, lawyers work for many different agencies but they are concentrated in the Departments of Justice, Treasury, and Defense. Other lawyers are employed as house counsel by public utilities, banks, insurance companies, real estate agencies, manufacturing firms, welfare and religious organizations, and other business firms and nonprofit organizations. Some salaried lawyers also have part-time independent practices; others work as lawyers part-time while working full-time in another occupation.

Education/Training

Admission to a state's bar—a lawyer's license—is a prerequisite to practice law in the courts of any state or jurisdiction. Nearly all states require that applicants for admission to the bar pass a written examination. Most jurisdictions also require applicants to pass a separate written ethics examination. Lawyers who have been admitted to the bar in one jurisdiction occasionally may be admitted to the bar in another without taking an examination, if they meet that jurisdiction's standards of good moral character and have a specified period of legal experience. Federal courts and agencies set their own qualifications for those practicing before them. To qualify for the bar examination in most states, an applicant must complete at least three years of college and also graduate from a law school approved by the American Bar Association (ABA) or the proper state authorities.

Although there is no nationwide bar examination, forty-seven states, the District of Columbia, Guam, the Northern Mariana Islands, and the Virgin Islands require the six-hour Multi State Bar Examination (MBE) as part of the bar examination; the MBE is not required in Indiana, Louisiana, Washington, and Puerto Rico. The MBE, covering issues of broad interest, is given in addition to a locally prepared six-hour state bar examination. The three-hour Multi State Essay Examination (MEE) is used as part of the state bar examination in a few states. States vary in their use of MBE and MEE scores.

It usually takes seven years of full-time study after high school—four years of undergraduate study followed by three years in law school—to complete the required education. Although some law schools accept a very small number of students after three years of college, most require applicants to have a bachelor's degree.

There is no recommended or required "prelaw" major. However, certain undergraduate courses give the student the skills needed to succeed both in law school and in the profession. These include English, a foreign language, public speaking, government, philosophy, history, economics, mathematics, and computer science.

Students interested in a particular aspect of law may find related courses helpful. For example, future tax lawyers should have a strong undergraduate background in accounting. Others may need courses in engineering or architecture.

Acceptance by most law schools depends on the applicant's ability to demonstrate an aptitude for the study of law, usually through good undergraduate grades, the Law School Admission Test (LSAT), the quality of the applicant's undergraduate school, and any prior work experience. Some law schools require a personal interview. Law schools vary in the weight that they place on each of these factors.

Career Mobility

Most beginning lawyers start in salaried positions, usually as research assistants to experienced lawyers or judges. After several years of progressively more responsible salaried employment, some lawyers are admitted to partnership in their firm, or go into practice for themselves. Some lawyers, after years of practice, become full-time law school faculty or administrators; a growing number have advanced degrees in other fields as well.

Some attorneys use their legal training in administrative or managerial positions in various departments of large corporations. A transfer from a corporation's legal department to another department often is viewed as a way to gain administrative experience and rise in the ranks of management. Some lawyers become judges.

Desired Characteristics

Lawyers must have excellent research and communication skills. They should like to work with people and be able to win the respect and confidence of their clients, associates, and the public. Integrity and honesty are vital personal qualities. Perseverance and reasoning ability are essential to analyze complex cases and reach sound conclusions. Lawyers also need creativity when handling new and unique legal problems.

Trial lawyers need an exceptional ability to think quickly and speak with ease and authority, and must be thoroughly familiar with courtroom rules and strategy.

Job Outlook

The Bureau of Labor Statistics projects 209,000 job openings for attorneys in the next decade, due to growth and net replacements. The increased demand for lawyers will result from growth in the population and the general level of business activities. Demand will also be spurred by growth of legal action in such areas as employee benefits, health care, intellectual property, sexual harassment, the environment, and real estate. Legal services can be expensive, but the availability of legal clinics and prepaid legal service programs should increase the use of legal services by middle-income groups.

Competition for job openings has been and will continue to be keen because of the large numbers graduating from law school each year. During the 1970s, the annual number of law school graduates more than doubled, outpacing the rapid growth of jobs. Growth in the yearly number of law school graduates tapered off during the 1980s, but again increased in the early 1990s. The high number of graduates will strain the economy's capacity to absorb them. Although graduates with superior academic records from well-regarded law schools will continue to enjoy good opportunities, most graduates will encounter competition for jobs. As in the past, some graduates may have to accept positions in areas outside their field of interest or for which they feel they are overqualified. They may have to enter jobs for which legal training is an asset but not normally a requirement. For example, banks, insurance firms, real estate companies, government agencies, and other organizations seek law graduates to fill many administrative, managerial, and business positions.

The willingness to relocate may be an advantage in getting a job, but to be licensed in a new state, a lawyer may have to take an additional state bar examination. In addition, employers increasingly seek graduates who have advanced law degrees and experience in a particular field such as tax, patent, or admiralty law.

Employment growth of lawyers will continue to be concentrated in salaried jobs, as businesses and all levels of government employ a growing number of staff attorneys, and as employment in the legal services industry is increasingly concentrated in larger

Median Salaries of Lawyers Six Months After Graduation, 1996

Type of Work	Median Salary
All graduates	$40,000
Private practice	50,000
Business/industry	45,000
Academia	35,000
Judicial clerkship	35,000
Government	34,500
Public interest	30,000

Source: National Association for Law Placement

law firms. The number of self-employed lawyers is expected to continue to increase slowly, reflecting the difficulty of establishing a profitable new practice in the face of competition from larger, established law firms. Also, the growing complexity of law, which encourages specialization, and the cost of maintaining up-to-date legal research materials favor larger firms.

Earnings

Median salaries of lawyers six months after graduation from law school in 1996 varied by the type of work.

Salaries of experienced attorneys also vary widely according to the type, size, and location of their employer. The median annual salary of all lawyers was about $60,000 in 1996. General attorneys in the federal government averaged around $72,700 a year in 1997; the relatively small number of patent attorneys in the federal government averaged around $81,600.

Lawyers who practice alone usually earn less than those who are partners in law firms.

The Passion Factor: What do you like most about your occupation?

"I like to go into court, argue cases, and be able to persuade the judge and jury—as I face an adversary who's just as prepared as I am—to advocate on my client's behalf," says attorney Martin Castro, who became interested in law because of his father.

Through his father, who was an elected official, Castro had the chance to meet many powerful people. "And they were all lawyers," he explains.

Related Occupations

Some occupations which require similar skills include paralegal, arbitrator, journalist, patent agent, title examiner, legislative assistant, lobbyist, FBI special agent, political officeholder, and corporate executive.

Additional Information

American Bar Association
750 N. Lake Shore Drive
Chicago, IL 60611

Law School Admission Council
PO Box 40
Newtown, PA 18940

Hispanic National Bar Association
1700 K Street NW, Suite 1005
PO Box 66105
Washington, DC 20035
(202) 293-1507
http://www.incacorp.com/hnba

The specific requirements for admission to the bar in a particular state or other jurisdiction may also be obtained at the state capital from the clerk of the Supreme Court or the administrator of the State Board of Bar Examiners.

Paralegals

The increased use of paralegals is driven by the need to save money. After all, these professionals can do many of the same things a lawyer does—at a fraction of the cost. However, paralegals working in law firms whose clients are largely Spanish monolinguals can help bring legal representation closer to the Latino community.

The Job

Lawyers are often assisted in their work by paralegals or legal assistants. They perform many of the same tasks as lawyers, except for those considered exclusive to the practice of law. Although lawyers assume responsibility for the legal work, they often delegate many of their tasks to paralegals. However, paralegals are prohibited from setting legal fees, giving legal advice, and presenting cases in court.

Paralegals generally do the preparatory work involved in closings, hearings, trials, and corporate meetings. They investigate the facts of cases to make sure that all relevant information is uncovered. They conduct legal research to identify the appropriate laws, judicial decisions, legal articles, and other materials that are relevant to assigned cases. Paralegals may prepare written reports that attorneys use to determine how cases should be handled. If attorneys decide to file lawsuits on behalf of clients, paralegals may help prepare the legal arguments, draft pleadings and motions to be filed with the court, obtain affidavits, and assist attorneys during trials. Paralegals also organize and track files of all documents and correspondence important to cases, and make them available to attorneys.

Paralegals may work in all areas of the law, including litigation, bankruptcy, corporate law, criminal law, employee benefits, patent and copyright law, and real estate. They help draft contracts, mortgages, separation agreements, and trust instruments. They may also help prepare tax returns and plan estates. Some paralegals coordinate the activities of other law office employees, and keep the financial records for the office.

Paralegals who work for corporations help attorneys with employee contracts, shareholder agreements, stock option plans, and employee benefit plans. They may help prepare and file annual financial reports, maintain corporate minute books and resolutions, and help secure loans for the corporation. Paralegals may also review government regulations to ensure the corporation operates within the law.

Depending on the agency they work for, paralegals employed in government generally analyze legal material for internal use, maintain reference files, conduct research for attorneys, collect and analyze evidence for agency hearings, and prepare informative or explanatory material on the law, agency regulations, and agency policy for general use by the agency and the public.

Paralegals employed in community legal service projects help the poor, the aged, and others in need of legal assistance. They file forms, conduct research, and prepare documents. When authorized by law, they may represent clients at administrative hearings.

In small- and medium-size law firms, some paralegals perform a variety of duties that require a general knowledge of the law. For example, they may research judicial decisions on improper police arrests or help prepare a mortgage contract. Those who work for large law firms, government agencies, and corporations tend to specialize in one aspect of the law. These include real estate, estate planning, family law, labor law, litigation, and corporate law. Within specialties, functions often are broken down further so paralegals may deal with a specific area. For example, paralegals specializing in labor law may deal exclusively with employee benefits.

A growing number of paralegals use computer software packages to do legal research on-line or through the Internet. In litigation involving many supporting documents, paralegals may use computer databases to organize, index, and retrieve the material. Imaging software allows paralegals to scan documents directly into a database. Paralegals sometimes use billing programs to track hours billed to clients. They may also use computer software packages to perform tax computations and explore the consequences of possible tax strategies for clients.

According to the Bureau of Labor Statistics, paralegals held about 113,000 jobs in 1996. The vast majority worked in private law firms; most of the remainder were employed in various levels of government. Within the federal government, the Department of Justice is the largest employer, followed by the Departments of Treasury and Defense, and the Federal Deposit Insurance Corporation. Other employers include state and local governments, publicly funded legal service projects, banks, real estate development companies, and insurance companies. A small number of paralegals contract their services to attorneys or corporate legal departments.

Education/Training

Formal paralegal training can be obtained through associate's or bachelor's degree programs, or certificate programs. Increasingly, employers prefer graduates of four-year paralegal programs, or college graduates who have completed short-term paralegal certificate programs. However, the majority of paralegals hold associate's degrees. Some employers prefer to train paralegals on the job, promoting experienced legal secretaries or hiring college graduates with no legal experience. Other entrants have experience in a technical field that is useful to law firms, such as tax preparation for tax and estate practice, or nursing or health administration for personal injury practice.

Paralegal training programs are offered by four-year colleges and universities, law schools, community and junior colleges, business schools, and proprietary schools. The requirements for admission to formal training programs vary widely. Some require some college courses or a bachelor's degree; others accept high school graduates or those with legal experience; and a few schools require standardized tests and personal interviews.

The quality of paralegal training programs varies; the better programs generally emphasize job placement. Paralegals do not need to be certified, but the National Association of Legal Assistants has established standards for voluntary certification requiring various combinations of education and experience.

Career Mobility

In large law firms, corporate legal departments, and government agencies, experienced paralegals may supervise other paralegals and clerical staff, and delegate work assigned by the attorneys. Advancement opportunities include promotion to managerial and other law-related positions within the firm or corporate legal department. However, some paralegals find it easier to move to another law firm when seeking increased responsibility or advancement. Others attend law school and become attorneys.

Desired Characteristics

These professionals must have excellent oral and written communications skills and must be able to handle legal problems logically. They also must understand legal terminology and have good research and investigative skills. Familiarity with the operation and applications of computers in legal research and litigation support is increasingly important.

Because paralegals often deal with the public, they must be courteous and uphold the high ethical standards of the legal profession. The National Association of Legal Assistants, the National Federation of Paralegal Associations, and a few states have established ethical guidelines paralegals must follow.

Job Outlook

The Bureau of Labor Statistics projects a need for 86,000 paralegals through the year 2006, due to growth and net replacements. Demand will be driven by a growing population which requires additional legal services, especially in areas such as intellectual property, health care law, international law, elder law, sexual harassment, and the environment. Thus, private law firms will continue to be the largest employers of paralegals. Law firms and other employers with legal staffs increasingly hire paralegals to lower the cost, and expand the availability and efficiency of legal services.

The growth of prepaid legal plans should also contribute to the demand for the services of law firms. A growing array of other organizations, such as corporate legal departments, insurance companies, real estate and title insurance firms, and banks will also hire paralegals.

Job opportunities for paralegals will expand even in the public sector. Community legal service programs—which provide assistance to the poor, aged, minorities, and middle-income families—operate on limited budgets. They will seek to employ additional paralegals in order to minimize expenses and serve the most people. Federal, state, and local government agencies, consumer organizations, and the courts should continue to hire paralegals in increasing numbers.

Earnings

The average annual salary of paralegals was $34,514 in 1997, according to the National Federation of Paralegal Associations.

The average annual salary of paralegal specialists who work for the federal government was about $44,400 in 1997.

Generally, paralegals who work for large law firms or in large metropolitan areas earn more than those who work for smaller firms or in less populated regions.

In addition to a salary, 64 percent of paralegals received an annual bonus, which averaged about $2,094 in 1997.

The Passion Factor: What do you like most about your occupation?

"First of all, I like the legal field," confesses Estela Juárez, a paralegal who specializes in depositions at a private law firm. "I like to deal with people, I like to argue, and I'm very stubborn."

Born in Puerto Rico, Juárez wants to help people who do not speak English. "I love the job," she continues. "I spend 70 percent of my time on the phone, speaking to our clients to make sure they are available for the depositions. I also need to explain to them what a deposition is."

Related Occupations

Some occupations that share skill sets with paralegals include: abstractors, claim examiners, compliance and enforcement inspectors, occupational safety and health workers, patent agents, police officers, and title examiners.

Additional Information

Standing Committee on Legal Assistants
American Bar Association
750 N. Lake Shore Drive
Chicago, IL 60611

National Association of Legal Assistants, Inc.
1516 S. Boston Street
Suite 200
Tulsa, OK 74119
http://www.nala.org

National Federation of Paralegal Associations
PO Box 33108
Kansas City, MO 64114
http://www.paralegals.org (jobs)

American Association for Paralegal Education
PO Box 40244
Overland Park, KS 66204
http://www.usajobs.opm.gov

International Opportunities

O ccupations in the international arena may seem like the most obvious choice for bilingual Latinos. But there are many factors to consider before packing your bags. A second language, while a tremendous advantage, is no longer enough to get a job abroad.

"Today, you have to have excellent skills—in marketing, engineering, or whatever your field may be," says Julie Sell, director of the international practice at the Chicago Group, a marketing consulting firm. "The employer needs to see what value you can add to their company."

Lolie Camacho, who recruits volunteers for the Peace Corps, agrees. "People are usually surprised. But between 85 and 90 percent of our programs require degrees," she points out. "And the degrees are getting more and more specialized."

That is why it is a good idea to have an occupation—and some experience—before you even attempt to market your resume with multinational companies.

From a business perspective, marketing, advertising, and promotions are good fields for jobs in Latin America. "Most of their economies have turned the corner," explains Sell. "People have more money to spend. Stores like Wal-Mart opened in several Latin American countries, and people began to change their buying habits. They need new ways to advertise.... They need the technical knowledge we have in the United States."

Exporting is also a growing area because the demand for U.S. products in Latin America is higher than in the past. Also, more U.S. companies are feeling comfortable doing business there since the political situation is less volatile than in the past.

Camacho adds that the Peace Corps has several initiatives for which they need accountants, experts in business development, and people with experience in business administration. Among the attributes her organization seeks in its candidates are strong leadership skills, ability to motivate others, to plan and organize, to manage yourself, and to investigate what needs to be done and come up with solutions.

Bonnie Koenig, president of the consulting firm Going International, adds that individuals who are successful in international careers are open to different points of view, look for the opinions people have in common, reach for a consensus, and have a background in negotiation.

"If you have those skills you must learn to sell them when you apply for an international job," she says. "They are invaluable."

In addition to speaking the language of the country, most employers value candidates who are familiar with several cultures. Koenig points out that there is a difference between multiculturalism and multinationalism. "You can have multiculturalism within one country, but the cultural differences are all within the same framework. We all see the same media and have a certain way of communicating."

The differences between one country and another—even within Latin America—are much more dramatic.

"The perception in this country is that everything in Latin America is the same," says Sell. "But you need to have an appreciation of the different cultures. For example, I know of a Guatemalan businessman who works for Gillette and was transferred to Argentina. He had a very difficult time adjusting to the culture there."

The key is to recognize and appreciate differences among our own Latino cultures. The ideal way to gain that experience is to spend some time traveling or living in the countries where you would like to work. If that is not possible, seek out Latinos from different cultures so you can observe the way they behave, their attitudes, how they respond to certain things, and what words or phrases in your culture are innocent but might not be acceptable in theirs.

"It is the only way in which you could test, for example, how a product that succeeded in Chile will play in Mexico," says Koenig.

Jerry Pinotti, a multinational spark plug distributor who teaches a class on international business at Chicago's MacCormac Junior College, says that a successful "internationalist" is also open to opportunities, is flexible and creative, and is not afraid of new situations. "Anyone who needs to have everything predetermined is not going to be happy in this field because there are very few rules."

If you feel you have what it takes to launch an international career, the experts suggest you take the following steps.

Do research to find local companies that do business with Latin America or with any country that might be of interest to you. Often, these companies hire people in the U.S., train them, and then send them overseas. "But start with a smaller company," Sell recommends. "You get much more responsibility and gain experience faster. So they might transfer you sooner. Big companies tend to box you in."

Most service-oriented companies, such as airlines, banks, and consulting firms have branches or franchises in foreign countries. In the manufacturing sector, many companies have factories in other countries or need people to distribute and market their goods in those nations.

Join international organizations that offer seminars and organize a variety of events. These include the International Trade Association, the World Trade Center, the international division of your state's Department of Commerce and Community Affairs, and the U.S. Department of Commerce. Through them, you can find out which companies in your area do international business, and what are the latest international trends for people in your line of work.

Check out nonprofit organizations that also offer their services overseas. These include the American Friends Service Committee and Save the Children. The library will have descriptions of them if you don't live near any of their branches.

Choose a country, find out what documents and work permits you need, and just move there. Sell did just that when she was twenty-four years old. "I had saved enough money and I had a plan," she recalls, referring to her move to Asia. "Eventually, I landed a job with the *Wall Street Journal* and they sponsored me."

As everyone who has worked abroad will agree, it is probably not enough to *visit* a country. To get acquainted with its culture, and to be able to do business there, it is necessary to *live* among its people for a period of time.

Additional Information

Association of Professional Schools of International Affairs
(APSIA)
1779 Massachusetts Avenue NW
Washington, DC 20036

Hoover's Handbook of World Business (Reference Press, updated yearly).